Miss Abigail's Guide to Dating, Mating, & Marriage

Classic Advice for Contemporary Dilemmas

Abigail Grotke

THUNDER'S MOUTH PRESS
NEW YORK

MISS ABIGAIL'S GUIDE TO DATING, MATING, AND MARRIAGE
Classic Advice for Contemporary Dilemmas

Published by
Thunder's Mouth Press
An Imprint of Avalon Publishing Group Inc.
245 West 17th Street, 11th Floor
New York, NY 10011

AVALON
publishing group incorporated

Copyright © 2006 by Abigail Grotke

First printing March 2006

Library of Congress Cataloging-in-Publication Data is available.

ISBN: 1-56025-835-7
ISBN 13: 978-1-56025-835-3

9 8 7 6 5 4 3 2 1

Book design by Maria Elias
Printed in the United States of America
Distributed by Publishers Group West

To my family, for being there when I've needed advice.

Contents

Introduction

Single, lonely, looking for love? Thinking hopeless thoughts right now, wondering how you can snag the attention of the opposite sex? Perplexed by the intricacies of modern-day rituals of dating? It's not surprising that many of you are overwhelmed. You may long for the good old days when a young man or woman's primary goal in life was to find a mate, settle down, and start a family. Well, times have changed, and you can no longer just knock on the door of your neighbor's house and find the boy of your dreams. Contemporary single gals and guys have to do more work to find true love, or to find a date at all for that matter, particularly with today's hectic lives. Online dating isn't always the answer—nor is waiting for the producer of a reality show to discover you and set you up with your ideal mate.

With all the challenges, it's only natural that you would turn to a self-help book for some words of wisdom and encouragement. Advice books have been available throughout the years to help women and men find companionship. The downside? A person could spend the better part of their adult life just *reading* about how to get a date. And in this day and age, who has the time?

Lucky for you, I've already done the work. I've locked myself in my library and consulted my collection of classic advice books—all from a simpler time—to glean the best tips to help you in your quest for love. The advice in this book is culled from my personal self-help book collection, which consists of almost a thousand titles that span from the 1820s to the 1970s and cover the age-old topics of dating, love, living together, marriage, health, beauty, puberty, sex, etiquette, house-keeping, and home economics.

Forever awkward in dating situations, and mystified to this day by makeup and hair styling, my love of old advice books began with the purchase of a fifty-cent book at a Salvation Army thrift store in Greensboro, North Carolina. *The Art of Dating* was a 1967 book for teens written by Evelyn Millis Duvall and published by the YMCA's Association Press. From that beginning, my obsession grew, and I discovered other books in thrift stores and used-book shops over the last twenty years. Since 1997, the advice has been finding new life on my Web site, http://www.MissAbigail.com, as I set out to help readers with their contemporary dilemmas by seeking advice from the classic books. And now, the best-of have been compiled into this book: *Miss Abigail's Guide to Dating, Mating, and Marriage*.

While the language in these quotes is often quaint and curious, the insights remain remarkably fresh. Although some of the advice was written for teenage girls and boys, and some for older audiences of either sex, the words are often ageless. No matter your age, if you're single and trying to meet people, you've likely got anxieties about getting someone's attention, about how to behave on a date, about what to wear, and about whether you should kiss on the first date—and it doesn't necessarily get any easier if you're twenty, thirty-five, or fifty. And in spite of the fact that most of the classic advice is written with male-female relationships in mind (unfortunately, any other sort of relationship was taboo back then), those of you into partners of your own sex can certainly take the advice to heart as well. Simply replace the he's with she's, or the girls with boys, and go for it!

Whatever your age or gender or personal preferences, here's your opportunity to experience the advice of the past as your parents, grandparents, and great-grandparents lived it. The advice presented here will help you learn how to make yourself dateable, how to meet people, how to ask someone out, how to distinguish the pros and cons of flirting and petting. You'll share the joys of falling in love, the heartache of a breakup. I'll help you cope with being single, and then, when the time comes, you'll be prepared to start over with someone new. And ultimately, once you do find a partner for life, you'll learn how to live happily ever after with the guy or gal of your dreams. In sharing these favorites of classic advice, I'll help you to navigate your contemporary dating, mating, and marriage dilemmas; because sometimes you have to look back to go forward.

—Miss Abigail
(Abigail Grotke)

Chapter One
Starting Out

Q Dear Miss Abigail:
I've heard all this talk about dating. What's the big deal?

A It's quite a big deal, indeed! But before we dive in to all the reasons why that is, a short primer will be appropriate to help explain the language of love. According to Merriam-Webster's handy-dandy online dictionary (http://www.m-w.com), the definition of *dating* is "a social engagement between two persons that often has a romantic character." To *court*, on the other hand, is a bit more serious: "to engage in social activities leading to engagement and marriage." Finally, to *woo* is defined, similarly, as "to sue for the affection of and usually marriage with." That's a bit too serious for this opening chapter, so we'll focus on courtship and dating right now, with a little teaser on wooing near the end of the chapter. Read on: the following will tell you what you need to know as you get started dating.

1967: Off to a Good Start

Dating is one of the most exciting periods of your
life. Suddenly, there are new horizons before you,   *great*
friendships flower, your personality blooms, and   *exhilaration,*
your sense of being a desirable person worthy of   *splendor, and*
affection becomes real. This is a time of great   *discovery*
exhilaration, splendor, and discovery. To live it fully is
to enjoy one of life's most delightful experiences.

To miss out on dating is a shame and a waste, especially when there
is still time to do something about it. Dating is an art, and like all arts
it must be cultivated to give results. Approach it with honesty, enthusiasm, energy, and it begins to take form. And soon you have answers
to the questions that were worrying you.

Long before you actually start dating, you dream about it. Wistfully, you
see other fellows and girls out together on dates, laughing, talking, going
places, having a seemingly effortless, wonderful time. Before you ever get a
date, you see yourself as the gallant hero or the glamorous heroine of a
romantic situation. You imagine all the right words and actions so easily, so
vividly, that you can hardly wait to start dating. Yet, somewhere inside you
anticipate the awkward moments when you will stand tongue-tied and
clumsy before some very special person, finding that dating is anything but
wonderful. And so you swing between eagerness and anxiety, impatient to
try your wings at one moment, and afraid of a takeoff in the next.

When you consider the nature of dating, this emotional see-sawing
is quite understandable. For dating fun is different from the fun a boy
has playing ball with the fellows or the joy a girl knows confiding in her
closest chum. In dating you are involved with persons of the other sex.
You are learning about these other special people. And in the process

you are also discovering a great deal about yourself. You are on the threshold of a new kind of experience that is grown-up, romantic, and full of promise for your life ahead as a full-fledged adult.

—Evelyn Millis Duvall, *The Art of Dating*

1964: What Is a Date?

Dating covers a wide territory. The word *date* is both a noun and a verb. Applied to social affairs, a date may be a person, an occasion, or a procedure. There are blind dates and steady dates, Dutch dates and double dates, big dates and little dates. A date is anything from a brief Coke where each pays for his own, up to attending a junior prom, or back down to "I'll meet you at the same place after algebra class."

Regardless of whatever it is, all dates have one thing in common. The chief objective is for two special individuals, one masculine and one feminine, to please each other. This part of a date has not changed. Only the exteriors are different.

—Betty Allen and Mitchell Pirie Briggs, *Mind Your Manners*

While you might laugh off the next author's concept of courtship and "American looseness" as old-fashioned, I wouldn't be so quick. Young folks today would be wise to pay heed to these cautionary ideas from the 1880s.

1886: Courtship

Courting, in the sense in which we use the word, is distinctly an American custom. The social laws of other civilized countries are such as to preclude the possibility of the almost unrestrained association of the sexes in youth which we see in this country. We do not offer this fact as an argument in favor of foreign social customs, by any means, although in this one particular they often present great advantages, since in the majority of instances other evils as great, or even greater, are encouraged. We mention the fact simply for the purpose of bringing into bold relief the evils of the characteristic American looseness in this particular.

almost unrestrained association of the sexes

—J. H. Kellogg, *Plain Facts for Old and Young: Embracing the Natural History and Hygiene of Organic Life*

Despite Mr. Kellogg, loose and not-so-loose Americans and others around the world are going to keep on courting each other. It's just human nature—as countless programs on television have shown us. To get a better idea of what this is all about, let's look at a romantic passage from the 1940s. Note the lovely use of the word "wooing" (one of my personal favorites) in this passage. Say it with me. Woo me, please. Wooo. Wooooo. Doesn't that make you want to try it out for yourself?

1940: Courtship—for the Man

For the young man, wooing must be a great adventure. It is a voyage of discovery and exploration. He discovers the hidden beauties in the character of the one he loves concealed behind the curtain of her modesty, or even unknown to her. He discovers her innocent whims, her buried wishes. Then, by compliments, little gifts, or thoughtful acts, he brings to her attention by a series of surprises the results of this voyage. . . .

I have perhaps overemphasized the danger of becoming a slave to passion, but one must not forget that there must be passion. There must be an imperious, driving force in back of all wooing. It should never be permitted to sink to the boresome fulfillment of a certain number of weekly or monthly calls, tiresome, restrained participation in ordinary social functions. Romance, to live, must not be caged in the atmosphere of tame domesticity, nor deprived of the opportunity to soar.

one must not forget that there must be passion

—Margaret Sanger, *Happiness in Marriage*

Now that we've gone over the basic concepts of what dating is, perhaps you are wondering why you might even want a "special someone" in your life. Here's a healthy look at both the pluses and the minuses of relationships. You must decide if it's right for you.

1938: The Value of Boy Friends

Why is it important for a girl to know boys and have the friendship of boys? In order to get taken to parties, and have plenty of dates and dance partners?

Those things may seem essential, but having boy friends should mean more than that. It is good for a girl to know boys and to learn to get along with them, because later she will need to know how to get along with men, whether her career is marriage or a vocation. Her life will be happier, no doubt, and her career more successful, if she understands something about the opposite sex, if she can grasp their viewpoint and learn how their minds work, and how they think and feel about things. Girls can learn from boys an honesty and straightforwardness that is more characteristic of them than of girls. And a girl may find in her friendship with intelligent boys a stimulating development of her own mind and ideas.

learn how their minds work

Like all good things, however, boy-and-girl friendship can be overdone. The girl who devotes all her time and thought to boys gets a narrow, warped slant on life. If she is too busy having dates with boys to have any time left for girls, and for her family and other friends, she is paving the way for unhappiness for herself. For while she may be well supplied with boy friends, she soon comes to feel that girls don't like her. She imagines that, out of envy of her popularity with boys, girls go out of their way to hurt her. The result is that she is standoffish and suspicious with girls, and presently it is really true that they don't like her.

Knowing boys and getting along with boys is part of your education for life. But not all. Keep your girl friends, too, and make your life and personality well balanced.

—Beatrice Pierce, *The Young Hostess*

Chapter Two

What's Happening to Me?

Q   Dear Miss Abigail:
I feel too awkward and weird to even try to date. What the
heck is happening to me?

A   If there's one thing that has remained a constant over the
years, it's puberty—the time when young people's bodies
catapult them into adulthood. While some approaches for
dealing with puberty have varied over the years, the changes
that you're going through happened to every adult you see
walking around. Yeah, sure, you're feeling strange now, but
you'll grow out of it. I promise. Here are some tips to help
you get through this rocky stage.

1904: Change at Puberty

Up to the age of puberty the main differences between the sexes are mental rather than physical. The girl is naturally more quiet and domestic than the boy. She shows the feminine trait of inviting attention indirectly. Quite young, also, the boy perceives that it is his part to make the advances.

At the age of puberty there comes a change—so marked a change, at times, as to be almost startling. Although there have been many disputes as to the reality of definite physiological and mental changes in man and woman measured by a limited cycle of years—for instance, seven—there is no doubt whatever that at about the fourteenth year in both the boy and the girl so complete a transformation takes place as to make of them new beings. In temperate climates both the boy and the girl then assume their specific sexual functions. Heretofore each has been a separate and independent individual and felt no special need of the other, except insofar as the normal social nature called for companionship. With the deepening of the voice and the hardening and expansion of the masculine muscles, with the swelling of the feminine breast and the rounding of every outline, with all that these changes imply, there comes a marked difference in the bearing of the sexes toward each other.

so complete a transformation takes place

—Mary Ries Melendy, *Vivilore: The Pathway to Mental and Physical Perfection.*

1937: Puzzled

Have you ever felt like a young aviator going out to test his spurs? Has that feeling of strain, of eagerness for thrills yet fear of the unknown ever come over you?

As you dream of life ahead of you, aren't you puzzled over a number of things? You have trained a little for life, yet you know that the real battles and tests are in the future. And you want to be coolheaded in facing them.

You want to know how to face this test of life. You want to know what this body of yours is for; you want to know your ship and its controls. No smashup within the enemy lines for you, but a list of proud victories. Perhaps a medal or two or a piece of white ribbon on your chest to prove that you came through the battle of youth pure.

Knowing about sex matters is not wrong. In fact it is necessary. Only the abuse of such knowledge is wrong.

—P. J. Bruckner, *How to Give Sex Instructions*

1922: From Child to Woman

Wonderful changes take place in the body of a girl in transition. She takes on a new form and new symmetry. Organs that have been dormant during childhood suddenly wake into life and activity. She becomes, not merely a person, but a woman. And with this change in her physical being come just as wonderful changes in her nature. She has new emotions, new thoughts, and new aspirations. She has a new view of life and takes a new course of action. It is as if she were in another world, so completely does she change. . . .

new emotions, new thoughts, and new aspirations

The child becomes a woman at last. Slipped into girlhood naturally, and just as naturally she will lay off girlish ways and settle into womanhood. Life will take on a more sober look, and she will see things more distinctly. Many of the admonitions and proofs that she received in her girlhood, and which seemed hard and unnecessary at the time, will now appear in their true light, and she will thank her guardians who gave them. Her cheeks will glow with embarrassment when she thinks of some of her girlish escapades, and become redder still when she thinks of some of the things she wanted to do but Mother would not permit. She will talk more quietly and laugh less boisterously. New feelings of responsibility will press in upon her. Life will look more earnest and serious than it used to do. She will wonder how she could ever have been so careless of consequences. Our child is now a woman, and her nature craves something more real and satisfying than the fleeting pleasures of youth.

—Mabel Hale, *Beautiful Girlhood*

One common concern for a girl going through puberty is the size of her breasts. So while you struggle with the initial embarrassment of training bras, know this: the key is to be happy with what you've got. It's more than a starter bra, it's the start of a wonderful relationship with your anatomy.

1956: Don't Worship Your Anatomy

"Oh, Dr. Crane, I am so mortified because I have such large breasts," other girls will tearfully exclaim. "Would it be safe for me to have a plastic surgeon remove part of my breasts?"

Yes, it is safe enough, but usually not warranted. Small breasts and full breasts are really an inconsequential element in the total mosaic of traits that comprise a charming personality. . . .

an inconsequential element in the total mosaic of traits

Many girls with perfect anatomical busts are a perfect "bust" on a date, so get wise to reality. Other girls with flat chests or very pendulous busts are popularity personified, with proposals of marriage by the dozen, and that is literally true!

If you repose such credulous belief in the magic of a normal bust, then you are almost sure to be disappointed, even if you resorted to plastic surgery. For that very yen to have the surgeon make you popular, indicates you fail to see clearly what constitutes charming femininity.

A girl can be charming and popular though she has a leg removed or a breast amputated.

Freckles and a pug nose and skinny legs, or thick ankles and big hips, don't exert more than a minor influence on your total rating as "date bait."

A cheery smile and a ready compliment for your male companion can get you an engagement ring much faster than the most publicized Hollywood bust. If you still disbelieve me, just visit the Marriage License window at your county courthouse and watch the applicants thereat. There probably isn't one Hollywood type of female among them per thousand. Count 'em for yourself and see!

—George W. Crane, *How to "Cash-In" on Your Worries*

Of great importance in feminine hygiene is the selection of the bandeau. These photos show various styles.

This type does not provide sufficient support for the bust.

Tight brassieres (center) flatten the breasts. The best type (below) provides correct uplift.

Zits: everyone's got 'em . . . but knowing as I do how tragic it feels when they first appear, I'm hoping these words from Lois Pemberton's classic *The Stork Didn't Bring You* will help in your personal search for clear skin. (By the way, don't believe anyone who says acne goes away once you hit adulthood. Lies, I tell you, lies!)

1965: Oh, Woe Is You

Saddest of all the adolescent crosses to bear, and one that often leaves big mental as well as physical scars, is ACNE. Very few boys or girls escape it, though some have milder and shorter sieges than others.

It does seem unfair, and why it's necessary no one knows—though maybe it's just one of nature's strange character-molding devices. Best you can do is keep your chin up and know that acne does depart eventually for good.

You may, of course, feel self-conscious over it and plan staying home when you want terribly to go someplace special. Well, don't. Don't let it destroy your confidence and composure, either.

If you're a complete mess with a bumper crop from the start, have Mother take you to a dermatologist, follow his advice, and apply his medications to the letter. Be sure to use only your own prescriptions and don't fool around experimenting with stuff that worked for somebody else. Everyone is an individual case, reacting differently to different treatment. What worked swell for Joe or Jane may just prove poison for you.

If, however, you're just one of the "regulars" with a normally healthy spattering, while you're putting up with the unsightly spots and curbing the desire to bury your head in the sand till they subside, you can help yourself a lot. First of all, avoid being emotional about its appearance.

Upsets only make matters worse, stirring up the circulation and increasing rather than decreasing the number of bumps. So keep calm, stay away from mirrors, and steer clear of company that insists on reminding you of it. . . .

upsets only make matters worse

A very good thing to bear in mind is: those bumps don't show to others nearly as much as you imagine they do. Because you are extra conscious and sensitive of them, you may feel they look big as all outdoors. They aren't pretty; none of us likes to even see them, much less have them. Medical science is doing lots to straighten them out in the way of new treatments and diet; and perhaps, someday, acne won't even be a part of growing up. But until then, there isn't much more you can do.

—Lois Pemberton, *The Stork Didn't Bring You: Sex Education for Teen-Agers*

Got lots of questions about puberty? Your friends might have interesting things to say on the subject, but have you thought about trying your parents? I know that what is going on with your body is hard to talk about, but you should trust your mom or dad and open up to them about what you're going through. Heck, your mom was a girl once, too, and I bet she remembers what it was like. What follows are some thoughts about parents and their role in educating their kids. I know, it sounds kind of stuffy, but it was written way back in 1910!

1910: The Teacher

The parent should be the ideal teacher. After a few years of preparation with lessons of reproduction in plants and birds and the like, the mother might tell the story of mother and babies when the child is about eight years old, an age when it is especially curious, and when it is likely to get misinformation from its companions.

As the child gets older it should receive other necessary lessons at the appropriate time; for instance, the mother teaches the girl about the menses, motherhood, social disease, and a pure mind; the father the boy about seminal emissions, self-abuse, continence, and social disease.

One great advantage of parent as teacher, is that the child is likely to make a confidant of him and not go elsewhere, when seeking information on these subjects, a benefit to the child which can scarcely be overestimated. For the child should be in confidential relations with someone to whom it turns freely for advice in such matters, and it is fortunate indeed if that confidant is a wise parent.

he must be wise and discreet

So clearly, the parent might be the ideal teacher. But for the purpose he must be wise and discreet, equipped with knowledge, understand and be in sympathy with his children, and be willing to do his duty by them.

—Philip Zenner, *Education in Sexual Physiology and Hygiene*

How to give
SEX
INSTRUCTIONS

**A GUIDE
FOR PARENTS, TEACHERS**
and Others Responsible
for the
TRAINING OF YOUNG PEOPLE
By
F. J. BRUCKNER, S. J.
With a
FOREWORD BY DANIEL A. LORD, S. J.

A QUEEN'S WORK PUBLICATION

As a girl grows older, the questions she puts to her mother may bring up mixed feelings; sometimes these may be difficult to bear, but it's oh-so-important to work through any discomfort, as the authors of *The Mother's Book* make clear.

1919: The Period of Choice

Another period in the girl's life is drawing near. There is a new bloom in her cheek, a new life to her lips, a soft light in her eyes. It is the springtime of her life. The sap is running high in the trees, and the blood is calling for its fulfillment.

Young men eye her daughter with favor, and while there is a pride in the mother-heart, there is fear also. She knows the purity and white wealth of her daughter's life, but so little of these strange suitors! Suppose they should take her daughter's all and give her poverty in return? Filch from her her beauty, her womanhood, her self-respect even, and in return give her—God only knows what. So, out of her fear is born courage and determination, and she draws her daughter to her side again, and they counsel together as women.

out of her fear is born courage and determination

—Caroline Benedict Burrell and
William Byron Forbush,
The Mother's Book

Chapter Three
Becoming Dateable

Q   Dear Miss Abigail:
      What can I do to make myself dateable?

A   Any person just starting out on the adventure that is dating
      wonders what he or she can do to make themselves likeable,
      approachable, and, of course, dateable. Alas, there is no one
      magic formula that will make this happen, but this section
      covers a variety of areas in your life that you'll need to fine-
      tune as you prepare for dating. First, we need to build up
      your self-confidence. Also important: a positive attitude,
      good manners, and good grooming. Of course, enthusiasm
      about the challenges ahead helps, too!

1967: Be Enthusiastic

Life attracts life. Your enthusiasm will go out
from you in ever widening circles to enchant
those who come within its seductive power.
Enliven your relationships by bringing in
fresh fuel to the fire. If your social contacts
have grown stale, introduce new and fascinating
subjects. Plan new activities. Create an atmosphere of merriment. The
unexpected can be amusing. Dress your days with gaiety so that later
when you take them out of the closet of memories you can say, "This
one was fun to wear."

create an atmosphere of merriment

— Ruth Tolman, *Charm and Poise for Getting Ahead*

Now let's read along as a favorite author of mine, Evelyn Millis
Duvall, describes how teenagers can make themselves more dateable.
Do you have your pencil and paper out? You might want to take
some notes.

1956: Becoming More Dateable

"What is the matter with me?" you may wonder
if you do not have dates. Everybody else seems
to be talking about their good times—what he
said and what she said, and then what they did.
It sometimes makes a boy or girl who is not
dating feel pretty much out of things. You may get to
wondering if there is something wrong with you that keeps you from
going places and doing things with the other sex. You may put on a big
act and pretend that you have special friends and admirers (as many of

"What is the matter with me?" you may wonder

the others do, too). But deep down inside you may be puzzled about what it takes to make friends, to get a date, and why some people seem to do it all so easily while others have to work so hard at it.

You can improve your own dateability by following a few simple rules. You are more dateable to the extent to which you are increasingly friendly and sincerely interested in others. Loyal friends, people truly interested in each other, are always good companions. You are a better date as you practice good grooming habits more conscientiously. You do not have to dress extravagantly or dazzle your date with your appearance. But both boys and girls become more interesting to each other when they have mastered the basic rules of cleanliness, appropriateness, and general attractiveness of appearance.

You become more dateable as you develop more and more interests outside yourself. The more things you can do and enjoy doing, the more you have to share with others. The more things that interest you, the greater your insurance against being bored or spending a dull evening. Dullness is within yourself, just as good times are. You make your dates what they are by your ability to enjoy a number of things with various kinds of people. As your interests grow, you too grow, to the point where you like to do so many things that you can have a good time in countless ways and in all sorts of circumstances.

—Evelyn Millis Duvall, *Facts of Life and Love for Teen-Agers*

As you consider some of the elements that might be holding you back from your personal best, perhaps you should also do a cleanliness check. A good sniff under the armpits should indicate whether you need to hop in the tub more often.

1916: Cleanliness of the Person

Dr. Galopin remarks that "love begins at the nose." An unpleasant odor always shows itself about the person of those who neglect the bath. Bad smells lead to aversion. Bad-smelling persons are exceedingly disagreeable companions. . . .

love begins at the nose

Not infrequently young people are seen with dirty ears and neck. A dirty neck and smiling face are not in harmony. Every lady owes it to herself to be fascinating; every gentlemen is bound, for his own sake, to be presentable; but beyond this there is an obligation to society, to one's friends, and to those with whom we may be brought in contact.
—Professor T. W. Shannon, *Nature's Secrets Revealed: Scientific Knowledge of the Laws of Sex Life and Heredity, or Eugenics*

Am I ready for School today ?

Is my **hair** *brushed*
Is my **face** *washed*
Are my **ears** *clean*
Are my **teeth** *brushed*
Is my **neck** *clean*
?

Are my **hands** *washed*
Are my **finger nails** *clean*
Have I a fresh **handkerchief**
?

Are my **clothes** *neat*
Are my **stockings** *clean*
Are my **shoes** *shined*
?

ask the looking glass

1956: If You Don't Date, Don't Think You Are Different

Would it surprise you to know that most high school students do not date regularly? And that great numbers graduate without having had a single date? If you seldom date, or not at all, you are not different from the majority of your classmates. There

no need to feel that you are socially a failure

is no need to feel that you are socially a failure if you do not date. This does not mean that you should not date or try to get dates if you want them. It means simply that there are lots of other boys and girls like yourself who do not date, either because they are not interested or because they do not know how to get dates. Remember that there are many years ahead after you graduate from high school.

—Irene E. McDermott and Florence Nicholas,
Living for Young Moderns

Every decent advice book contains a quiz or two to get you thinking about how you might behave in certain situations. So get those pencils sharpened again, because being liked is a most wonderful thing, and I sure want all of you to be as likeable as you possibly can be so we can move on to the fun parts of dating. This self-analysis tool was published in Estelle Hunter's Personality Development Series. It may not automatically lead to popularity, but it can't hurt to give it a try.

1939: Do People Like You?

Every normal, healthy individual wants to be liked by others. If you have ever said that you didn't care whether or not people liked you, you probably weren't really honest with yourself. Perhaps you were trying to cover up hurt pride. The person who says bitterly, "I don't care," really does care a great deal. He should face the fact squarely and try to discover the reason for lack of harmony in his relationships with others.

Donald A. Laird, after a series of experiments made in the Colgate Psychological Laboratory to determine what traits were of most importance in making people liked or disliked, compiled the list of forty-five questions which is quoted on the following page.

TRAITS WHICH MAKE US LIKED

Give yourself a score of 3 for each of these questions to which you can answer "Yes":

1. Can you always be depended upon to do what you say you will?
2. Do you go out of your way cheerfully to help others?
3. Do you avoid exaggeration in all your statements?
4. Do you refrain from being sarcastic?
5. Do you refrain from showing off how much you know?
6. Do you feel inferior to most of your associates?
7. Do you refrain from bossing people not employed by you?
8. Do you keep from reprimanding people who do things that displease you?
9. Do you refrain from making fun of others behind their backs?
10. Do you keep from domineering others?

Give yourself a score of 2 for each of these questions to which you can answer "Yes":

11. Do you keep your clothing neat and tidy?
12. Do you avoid being bold and nervy?
13. Do you refrain from laughing at the mistakes of others?
14. Is your attitude toward the opposite sex free from vulgarity?
15. Do you keep from finding fault with everyday things?
16. Do you let the mistakes of others pass without correcting them?
17. Do you loan things to others readily?

Do you avoid being bold and nervy?

18. Are you careful not to tell jokes that will embarrass those listening?
19. Do you let others have their own way?
20. Do you always control your temper?
21. Do you keep out of arguments?
22. Do you smile pleasantly?
23. Do you refrain from talking almost continuously?
24. Do you keep your nose entirely out of other people's business?

Give yourself a score of 1 for each of these questions to which you can answer "Yes":

25. Do you have patience with modern ideas?
26. Do you refrain from flattering others?
27. Do you avoid gossiping?
28. Do you refrain from asking people to repeat what they have just said?
29. Do you avoid asking questions in keeping up a conversation?
30. Do you avoid asking favors of others?
31. Do you refrain from trying to reform others?
32. Do you keep your personal troubles to yourself?
33. Are you natural rather than dignified?
34. Are you usually cheerful?
35. Are you conservative in politics?
36. Are you enthusiastic rather than lethargic?
37. Do you pronounce words correctly?
38. Do you look upon others without suspicion?
39. Are you energetic?

40.   Do you avoid borrowing things?

41.   Do you refrain from telling people their moral duty?

42.   Do you refrain from trying to convert people to your beliefs?

43.   Do you refrain from talking rapidly?

44.   Do you refrain from laughing loudly?

45.   Do you refrain from making fun of people to their faces?

The higher your score by this self-analysis, the better liked you are in general. Each "No" answer should be changed through self-guidance into a "Yes" answer. The highest possible score is 79. About 10 percent of people have this score. The lowest score made by a person who was generally liked was 56. The average young person has a score of 64. The average score of a person who is generally disliked is 30. The lowest score we found was 12.

From these questions it is apparent that whether you are liked or disliked depends chiefly upon your attitude toward others. All your efforts at self-improvement will be of no avail if you think only of building up your own superiority. The consciously superior, the self-righteous person is never popular. If you would be liked, don't try to impress the other person with your importance; make him feel important; show your interest in him.

—Estelle B. Hunter, *Personality Development: A Practical Self-Teaching Course, Unit One: Your Physical Self*

So, how'd you do? In case anyone was wondering, my score was 59. I suppose I've got a bit of improving to do, haven't I? I'd better get to work!

Manners are crucial to likeability, and are something that should be
learned very early on; unfortunately, many today have somehow missed
out on this instruction. This 1822 poem for schoolchildren provides a
quick refresher for us all. Isn't it nice to know that picking your nose is
not just a modern problem?

1822: In Company

Intrude not where you're not desired,
Nor stay till everyone is tired.
Writhe not your limbs in every shape
Of awkward gesture, like an ape,
Nor twirl your hands, nor hit your toes—
Nor hum a tune—nor pick your nose—
Nor keep in motion as you sit,
Nor on the floor or carpet spit,
But in the fire with prudent care.
Nor lean upon another's chair.
If you must cough, or sneeze, be still
In doing it, if possible.
If you must yawn, just turn aside,
And with your hand the motion hide.
And when you blow your nose, be brief,
And neatly use your handkerchief.
All whispering, giggling, squinting shun,
Don't turn your back on anyone.
Nor bite your nails, nor lolling stand,
Nor in your pockets keep your hand.
Do not allow yourself to look

*all whispering,
giggling,
squinting shun*

In letters, papers, or a book,
'Till you have leave. If one is reading,
Don't overlook him; 'tis ill breeding.
Don't wear a frown upon your face;
Let cheerfulness your aspect grace.
To your superiors always strive,
In walking, your right hand to give.
A proper distance keep in mind,
Crowd not too near, nor lag behind.
To equals let your conduct be
Marked with sweet affability.

—Nancy Sproat, *The School of Good Manners*

Something else that may affect approachability is shyness, considered by some to be a terrible affliction. You may not believe it, but I was once a very shy girl myself. I can't recall exactly what brought me out of my shell (maybe it was performing French horn solos in band, or the need to stick up for myself when my little sister picked on me), but I'm here to make sure that you, too, will grow into a confident young man or woman. So, are you ready to ditch those fears and go out there and conquer the world? Now is as good a time as any.

1925: Shyness

Another defect girls often have which drives desirable men away is shyness, and very few people stop to analyze its cause. . . . If you are shy, take yourself sternly to task, analyze what makes you so, and overcome it. Bashfulness and

take yourself sternly to task

shyness are as great faults as boldness, and perhaps cause more unhappiness. The antithesis of shyness is bumptiousness, and this also comes from egotism; it is a different expression of the same fundamental fault. Try to eradicate the root if you have a tendency to either of its demonstrations.

—Elinor Glyn, *This Passion Called Love.*

Lillian Eichler wrote *Book of Etiquette* in 1921, and in 1922 the companion book *Etiquette Problems in Pictures* was published after she "[realized] the need for a picturization of the more unexpected blunders in etiquette," as the introduction explains. Eichler's texts were accompanied by illustrations by F. McAnelly that allowed readers to "see how you look when you are actually making the mistake." It's like looking into a mirror!

1922: Unhappy Wallflowers

The considerate hostess always invites more men guests than women, to obviate the possibility of unhappy wallflowers. But the young lady opposite is making a mistake. If she knew how to act, how to conduct herself, she would not be making herself a conspicuous wallflower.

obviate the possibility of unhappy wallflowers

The woman who is not asked to dance should launch into an interesting conversation with the matrons who usually sit in a group during the dance. She may talk about books, music, the drama—anything she pleases. If she remains by herself, she will be an obvious wallflower; but if she joins the other women who do not dance and chats with them, the embarrassment will be avoided.

The most attractive woman will lose her charm if she is sullen, shy, self-conscious. The young woman pictured here should not be brooding by herself, waiting for someone to come for her. She should be mingling with the other guests, making herself affable and agreeable.

—Lillian Eichler, *Etiquette Problems in Pictures*

A bit of reserve may be alluring, but too much standoffishness turns into a challenge when people are trying to meet one another. Let this, from Ella Wheeler Wilcox's *Men, Women and Emotions,* serve as a warning:

1897: Unapproachable People

There is a prevalent idea that people who are distant and unapproachable in demeanor are immensely valuable when their intimacy is once obtained. Hard to get acquainted with is supposed by many to be synonymous with "deep," "cultivated," and "worthy," when applied to character. So far as personal observation and experience goes, I have proven this idea to be utterly without foundation. A haughty exterior more frequently hides an empty head and heart than any profound quality.

"She is very deep; you will find her worth cultivating," was said to me once of an "unapproachable" woman whose "keep-off-the-grass" attitude had repelled me at first meeting. I devoted myself to a search for her hidden worth, but after many months I found her to be like one of those sterile New England farmlets where a fresh crop of stones appears as soon as the old ones are uprooted. Who does not recall a pounded thumb and wasted temper in his youth, trying to break the shell of a tough walnut, only to find a dried and shriveled meat within? As we advance in life we save our thumbs and our tempers by choosing the yielding almond and pecan and letting the doubtful walnut alone. Life is too short to waste it in such a difficult and often disappointing achievement.

trying to break the shell of a tough walnut

—Ella Wheeler Wilcox, *Men, Women and Emotions*

Boys, I know that you worry about being liked, too, even though you probably don't admit this freely. Particularly in front of girls. Well, I want you to know that you can always tell Miss Abigail if you're fretting about your likeability. With that in mind, here's one for you, junior:

1940: Let's Take a Slant at the Girls

I suppose that some of your substantial friendships are with girls— friendships that prompt you to comb your hair, press your pants, and create in you the desire to make yourself worthy of their respect. . . . Their natural intuition guides them in their admiration or dislike for others, to such an extent that any boy should feel honored if he has gained the respect and friendship of a nice girl.

There are many ways, son, to gain and hold their friendship. Let's dismiss the idea that girls admire only the "looks" of a boy. "Handsome is as handsome does," you know, and ten to one it's what the boy *does* that makes the impression. If you expect people to like you, above all be genuine, be yourself, and don't pose in imitation of others.

Remember, son, a gentleman can have as much fun as the next fellow. He can be a rowdy or a clown—all in the proper time and place—and still be one; it all depends on knowing *when* and *how* to draw the line in personal behavior.

a gentleman can have as much fun as the next fellow

If you expect girls to see your own good qualities, don't have your amusement at the expense or embarrassment of others; because sometimes for the sake of getting a laugh, you may antagonize or *hurt* one who will always remember it against you. Just soft-pedal on your criticism of others and don't belittle their efforts in a girl's presence as your *own* faults may loom larger than ever in the very act of discrediting others.

—Louis LeClaire Jones, *Birthday Chats with Tomorrow's Man*

Girls, you might be wondering why those boys are acting so weird all of a sudden. Well, they're trying to figure out how to interact with your kind. In the meantime, you might want to read Ellen Peck's simple explanation:

1969: What a Teenage Boy Is Like

A teenage boy is basically insecure. It all started when you were twelve and he suddenly noticed that you were wearing a bra. That's all the evidence he needed that you were definitely and completely *female*. But you left him feeling very unsure of himself as a *male*. Especially when you started acting giggly and embarrassed whenever he came around. (Yes, you did, too.) And that nice, comfortable feeling he had with you—and with all girls when *they* looked pretty much like *he* did—changed. You became different then. Because of that bra, and the giggly behavior, he began to feel uncomfortable and tongue-tied around you. And maybe he isn't quite over that feeling yet. Even though you've stopped the giggling. (Or, if you haven't, do.)

when you started acting giggly

—Ellen Peck, *How to Get a Teen-Age Boy and What to Do with Him When You Get Him*

Have you ever had a beautiful friend that overshadowed you? Someone whom all the boys seemed to fawn over and ask out regularly, while you sat in the shadows waiting for someone to notice you? Well, there's no need to feel jealous any longer. It's not beauty that counts, it's *loveliness*. As author Kay Thomas says in the foreword to her book *Secrets of Loveliness*: "Not every girl can be beautiful. Beauty is a quality that a special few are born with. But loveliness, the aim of all women through the ages, can be acquired. The secrets of loveliness can be learned."

Ms. Thomas offers up some advice that might be of use to you in the following:

1964: Be Yourself

Even though you're trying to grow and develop and change (for the better!), always try to be yourself. Does this sound contradictory? It's not, really. It just means: Don't try to pretend you're someone you're not or haven't yet become. It just means: Don't pretend you're rich if you're poor, or sophisti-

fake behavior creates a strain

cated if you're inexperienced, or dumb if you're smart—as some girls do in the mistaken idea that this kind of play-acting is a good way to gain friends or get dates. (Next time you hear that boys don't like girls with brains, take a look at the girl who's saying so. Is she by chance bright and unpopular, and looking for an excuse for her lack of dates?)

This kind of fake behavior creates a strain that gets in the way of the very friendship you're trying to promote.

So be yourself. However, this doesn't mean standing still. It does mean that instead of pretending to have someone else's qualities, you could stretch some of your own. Instead of trying to act sophisticated, which you're not, act more considerate, which you can be. In other words, be your *best* self.

—Kay Thomas, *Secrets of Loveliness*

1939: Personality

Get a line. Have some individuality that will make you stand out from the crowd. Don't copycat other girls. Be yourself. Be natural. Don't pose. There is no other girl in the world less attractive to men than the affected one.

Remember that while some men like wild girls, others prefer prim little Puritans; that while some men like chatterers others like the soft, silent, smiling Mona Lisa; and that while some men like girls who can mix cocktails most men want wives who can bake cakes like Mother used to make. So stick to your own line of attractions and put the loud pedal on that instead of trying to crab some other girl's act.

while some men like wild girls others prefer prim little Puritans

—Dorothy Dix, *How to Win and Hold a Husband*

Chapter Four

I Like This Boy but I Don't Know How to Tell Him

Q Dear Miss Abigail:
There is this really cute, sweet guy I like, and but I can't tell if he likes me back. He talks to me a lot and smiles and makes me laugh, but I don't know if that means anything. Please, I need your help!

A If Miss Abigail had a frequently asked questions list, this would top it. Whether it's from a girl with a crush on a boy, or a boy with a crush on a girl, this certainly seems to be the biggest problem out there. My gut reaction is: "Well, say something! Tell him you like him!" or, "Go ahead, tell her you think she's cute!" But as we all know, that's easier said than done. And if it were easy to do, advice columnists would be out of business. What's the answer? This chapter will guide you through this asking-out period, which includes meeting someone, expressing feelings to them, and maybe, just maybe, asking them out.

Where to begin? I bet you never thought that a silly little rhyme could help you meet a date. Well, it can. Here's a little refresher course in introductions and taking that first step toward L-O-V-E. Though the approach may be, um, unique, you might be surprised how much it can help.

1946: Getting Under Way

I hear you say, "My trouble is not too many dates, or going after other people's dates, or giving up dates. My trouble is getting under way in the first place." The strategic thing is the introduction. . . . Introductions must be exploratory, both must share the exchange of remarks which follow. The talk must be small, very small and light. If there hasn't been any hint given to act as a starter of conversation, you'll just have to look about you and fasten upon anything that offers itself, even a tiny spider.

At a porch party two newcomers who had just been introduced caught sight of a little spider on the railing. Instead of screaming and acting silly the girl quickly chanted:

> *"Oh, a peeny, weeny pider*
> *Went up a water pout.*
> *Down came the rain*
> *And washed the pider out."*

"Is there any more?" asked the boy.
"Oh, yes;

> *Out came the sun*
> *And dried up the rain,*
> *And the peeny, weeny pider*
> *Went up the pout again."*

Then of course the boy had to take a try at it with the resulting laughter as his piders and pouts got all mixed up. Silly? Yes, silly, but funny-silly. It's that kind of thing that brings a first date.

silly, but funny-silly

—Frances Bruce Strain, *Teen Days: A Book for Boys and Girls*

Guys: afraid to ask the gals out? I'll tell you what you can do. Head to a bookstore and see if you can find yourself a copy of Eric Weber's "World-Famous" *How to Pick Up Girls!* "Over 600,000 Copies Sold!

New, Enlarged Edition! Featuring Interviews and Photos of Beautiful Girls! The World's Fastest, Easiest Way to Meet New Women!" claims the cover of this book (my version was published in 1970, though it is still in print today). Eric Kibble, from *Pick Up Times*, raves: "*How to Pick Up Girls* stands alone, unrefuted, authoritative. . . . It is a masterpiece." What more could you want?

1970: No Time Like the Present

There's going to be lots of times in the next few weeks when some super-dynamite girl saunters by. And you're going to think to yourself, "Now there's someone I'd exchange both of my big toes for. I'm going to pick her up."

But then a very strange thing happens. Just as you're getting all ready to approach her, you don't feel like it anymore. You tell yourself, "Now isn't really the time. I need more experience. More practice. Tomorrow I'll pick someone up. I'm just not in the right mood today."

If and when you find yourself telling yourself lies like these I urgently urge you to demand of your- *cut the* self to cut the crap. When it comes to picking up *crap* girls there's no time like the present. Do not delay or you'll find yourself delaying all your life.

Do not procrastinate or you'll see one girl after another waltz right out of your life. Picking up women is not that hard or complicated. With a little spontaneity and courage you'll surprise the hell out of yourself.

Next time you find yourself making excuses not to take action, get angry. Tell yourself this can't go on. Tell yourself, I've got to take action.

And do it. Take action. Right then and there. Say anything. Tell the girl she's got a look in her eyes that makes you weak in the knees. Tell her you love the coat she's wearing. Tell her anything. But make contact. Because once you do, nine-tenths of the battle is done.

Figure it this way. If you try and muff, you'll feel better than if you never tried at all.

You'll feel braver. You'll feel at least you gave it your best.

—Eric Weber, *How to Pick Up Girls!*

Still feeling a little shy about meeting girls? Wondering what to say? What to do? Frozen with fear? "Open up that mind, son, and snap into things," says author Louis LeClaire Jones. If I were you, I'd listen to him.

1940: Nerve vs. Confidence

You may have a girl friend whom you admire from a distance. It's "from a distance" because you haven't the courage to treat her as a friend, much as you would like to. To tell the truth she may be quite anxious to know you better, but your timidity is mistaken for cool- ness, and perhaps the chance for a fine friendship is lost because of it. It may surprise you to discover how cordially you would be received if you would turn down that inferiority idea for a while, and ignore its existence by denying it to yourself.

approach the problem with a calm, serene feeling of assurance

There is a difference between "nerve" and "confidence." Nerve is something you use to force a situation—while confidence comes by honestly and fairly acquiring, through experiment and experience, the courage to accomplish what you set out to do. When a fellow acts on his *nerve* it is with the feeling that he is attempting something beyond him, but hopes he will succeed. When you do a similar thing in *confi- dence*, you approach the problem with a calm, serene feeling of assur- ance which denies any thought of failure. Son, if you don't meet that girl, maybe you lack a little of both, and because of a certain "complex" which has you "buffaloed!"

    —Louis LeClaire Jones, *Birthday Chats with Tomorrow's Man*

1956: Asking

Asking for a date is simpler if the boy realizes he is just giving an invitation, and all invitations should be cordial and definite. So a boy should smile and act in a friendly manner when he asks for a date. He should also be exact and to the point. The girl will like it when her would-be date says, "The Christian film *A Greater Challenge* is to be shown at the Richmond Avenue Church Friday night. Would you like to go?" Such an invitation tells the girl "When" and "Where." It helps her to decide whether she can accept the date.

be exact and to the point

Boys should avoid the question approach, such as, "What are you doing Saturday afternoon?" Maybe the girl isn't doing anything, but she hesitates to say so until she knows what the boy has in mind.

—Clyde M. Narramore, *Life and Love: A Christian View of Sex*

Let's say you've gotten up your courage, and you're ready to ask out the girl you've been admiring. Here are some tips to help you navigate the process.

1967: Be Courteous

As you ask a girl for a date, you should indicate that you really want to go out with her. Courtesy is very important when asking, for if the girl finds you are not too courteous on the phone, she may assume you're also discourteous on dates. A typical phone call for a date might be something like this:

MARY: Hello.

JIM: Hi, Mary, this is Jim Jones.

MARY: Hi, Jim, how are you?

JIM: Fine, thanks. Say, did you understand that problem in math today? I found it rather confusing.

MARY: I did, too, but I eventually figured it out.

JIM: So did I. Say, Mary, Bob and Larry are taking Jean and Jane to the White Kar roller skating rink this Saturday—about seven o'clock. I'd like very much to take you, and we'd be home by ten. Would you like to go?

MARY: It sounds like fun! I'd love to go skating with you, Jim. I'll expect you Saturday about seven.

JIM: Fine, see you then. Good-bye, Mary.

MARY: Good-bye.

This conversation was a great help to Mary. She knows everything she needs to know. Mary knows that Jim really wants to take her skating. She knows that she should dress casually, and that she should be ready by seven. She can tell her parents that she will be home by

this is the kind of invitation she likes to receive

ten. This is the kind of invitation she likes to receive, because nothing is left up in the air. He told her who he was at once, instead of playing childish "Guess-who-this-is" games. No girl likes to admit that she doesn't recognize a boy's voice, yet many voices sound similar over the phone.

Mary's parents like this approach, too. They know just what they can expect without having to quiz Jim when he comes to pick her up for the date. They like to know where their daughter is going and with whom, but they hate to give a boy the third degree before a date—just as much as a boy hates to get it.

Jim also feels happy about this conversation. He knows that Mary will be dressed for skating, and that her parents understand about the arrangements. He can also tell his parents when to expect him home. Dates with arrangements agreed on ahead of time are more fun. You can look forward to your plans, rather than wonder what you're going to do and whether you'll be dressed appropriately.

—Evelyn Millis Duvall, *The Art of Dating*

1961: Cool Ways to Ask for a Date

DON'T WASTE TIME

If you've met a girl who interests you, don't brood about it and spend weeks getting up the courage to ask for a date. By the time you're ready, she may have forgotten how delightful you are. Ask when the urge hits you. That's now.

BE STRAIGHTFORWARD

Call her up, ask her how she is, etc., and before more than one minute has elapsed in idle conversation, pop the question you called about: *ask when* "Would you like to go to the movies with me *the urge* on Saturday night?" You'll get a quick yes or *hits you* no, and you'll avoid all that tentative beating around the bush which often proves to be so nerve-wracking. Sure, there'll be some rejections. And also some unexpected acceptances. In the long run, you'll find they balance out and you'll be a lot calmer in your dating life. And more natural.

CAVEMAN APPROACH

Dash over to her, grab her by the hair, and say: "Honey, you're coming to the show with me tonight!" Better have a twinkle in your eye . . . and be prepared for a fist in the same spot.

BE YOURSELF

If you can bear it, chances are that she can, too.

—Art Unger, *The Cool Book: A Teen-Ager's Guide to Survival in a Square Society*

Well, well. We've heard all this talk of boys asking girls out. What about girls who make the first move? While there isn't a whole lot of information in the classic advice arena regarding this alternative approach, there is some hope that young ladies can feel confident in taking charge of their destiny. Ellen Peck's girl-positive advice from the fabulous *How to Get a Teen-Age Boy and What to Do with Him When You Get Him* covers this topic. Apparently, if you don't make it easy for them, it'll never happen. Those silly boys.

1969: Make That First Move Yourself!

It will . . . be easier to become more outgoing if you stop worrying about whether people (boys) are going to respond or not. Forget any possible consequences of rebuff—or gossip—and *make that first move yourself!*

You smile first. You wave first. You talk first. If you stand around like a statue waiting for him to make the first move, you could collect a lot of dust! You should be down off your pedestal making contacts and saying "Hi"'s. And it's up to *you*, not him. The *worst* advice ever is, "Be ladylike. Don't be forward. Wait for him to speak to you. He will when he's ready."

it's up to you, not him

Ridiculous. We need to get rid of the "ladylike" myth if it means standing around like a stone. Get rid of the idea that making the first move with a boy is unfeminine. It's *very* feminine. It ought to be fairly obvious that women, as a sex, at all ages, all over this planet, have one similar job: to make things easy for men. Women type men's letters, cook their meals, keep their houses, plan their parties, iron their shirts, and in general make their life pleasant. *Why*, then, leave the strain of starting a conversation to a guy? It just doesn't make sense. Especially since you are more ready than he is to talk and know more about *how* to talk. . . .

You could be rebuffed. Sure, this does happen. . . . When and if this happens, of course, cover with this one-liner: "Oh, really?"

Deliver those two words with a chin-up, so-what smile and walk away. This little phrase is magic. It answers any comment—no matter what the comment was—and leaves the boy trying to figure out just what you meant and how he should interpret it. In other words: you walked away with the upper hand.

Keep in mind that it's the guy who's ill at ease with girls who may put you off, sometimes without meaning to. The "Oh, really?" is especially perfect for him. It hasn't completely closed the door (as a rude remark would have) and so, in case this guy grows up later, you might end up getting to know him yet.

Even if—and just for the heck of it, let's imagine the very worst ghost in anybody's closet—a guy says, "Hey, get lost. Leave me alone." Deliver your "Oh, really?" line and walk off to some friends and say, "Hey, what a *grouch* I just ran across!"

Which he is. *He's* got problems. *You* haven't.

—Ellen Peck, *How to Get a Teen-Age Boy and What to Do with Him When You Get Him*

1940: Calls

Modern young people call each other up for crisp little breezy messages, jokes, or invitations. Girls of the last generation did not call young men on the telephone, but waited until they were called. Today's straightforward girl would just as soon call a boy to tell him or ask him something as she would her grandmother. She would not, however, call him and say in a silly,

truly admirable and very refreshing

honeyed voice, "What are you doing this evening—why don't you ever come to see me?" Neither would she hang on the telephone and purr and coo into it, wheedling him into some attention to her. She would frankly and cheerfully ask him to do whatever she wanted him to do, if it did not interfere with his duties or studies or his preparation for the next day's demands. And he would just as cheerfully accept or refuse her request. There's something clean-cut and downright about these young moderns that is truly admirable and very refreshing.

—Margery Wilson, *Pocket Book of Etiquette*

Just because someone asks you out doesn't mean you have to accept the offer. An important part of dating is learning how to turn someone down politely (and, on the other side, how to accept rejection graciously!). So, as a responsible advice giver, I also include this tip:

1956: When You Don't Want to Date

It is discourteous for a boy to ask why when a girl tells him that she cannot do something that he asks. When a boy pushes for explanation of a girl's refusal, she is justified in kidding him about his persistence, or in simply changing the subject.

refuse his attentions courteously

If a girl does not ever want to date a particular boy, she does him a kindness when she gives him no encouragement whatsoever. To lead a boy on, when she never intends to go out with him, does him an injustice and unnecessarily prolongs the refusals. There are many reasons that a girl may refuse to consider dating a particular boy. He may drink, or run around with a fast set, or have a bad reputation, or be the kind of person whom for other reasons she does not feel she can associate with. If he is not dateable from her point of view, she will be wise to refuse his attentions courteously but with firmness and finality.

—Evelyn Millis Duvall, *Facts of Life and Love for Teen-Agers*

1922: Conduct toward Men

Male acquaintances should be carefully chosen, and great care exercised in accepting invitations from them.

When declining invitations from a man personally given, explanations are not necessary. If they are deemed desirable, they should be given as delicately as possible and without giving offence.

—W. C. Green, *The Book of Good Manners: A Guide to Polite Usage for All Social Functions*

Duvall's advice aside, I'll assume you're a "go" with this dating thing, and that you'd like to pursue (or be pursued by) a certain guy or gal. So now it's time for the next step—learning to flirt!

Chapter Five

The Fine Art of
Flirtation

Q Dear Miss Abigail:

Seriously, though, I'm desperate. Sure, others have asked me out, but the guy I've got my eye on hasn't given me a second glance. How can I get his attention?

A Ever heard of a little something called flirting? It comes naturally to some, but for many it's a skill to be learned and improved upon as relationships with others are explored. Let's start with some tips for making yourself alluring from Dorothy Dix's *How to Win and Hold a Husband.* Your flirtatious, fabulous self is on the line!

1939: Lures Men Can't Resist

We must not overlook those certain charms and wiles to which practically all men are susceptible. If you will cultivate these you will be fairly sure of never being dateless and of eventually making the grade to the altar with the youth of your choice. These are:

THE COME-HITHER LOOK IN THE EYE. A sort of come-on look, if you get what I mean. A look that subtly indicates to a man that a girl regards him as a great big wonderful sheik and that she is having the time of her life when gazing worshipfully up into his eyes.

No boy is going to see a girl a second time who high-hats him. No boy is going to make love to a girl who is as unresponsive as a stone image. If there ever was a time when men ran after the women who flouted them, it is out now. The modern man has to be lured into love. He doesn't break in of his own accord. . . .

don't feed men flattery in hunks, with a shovel

THE FINE ART OF JOLLYING. Don't feed men flattery in hunks, with a shovel. They resent this. But every man will eat out of your hand if it is filled with sugar. Don't be a crude bungler and tell a man in so many words that he is God's masterpiece. Get the idea across to him in other ways—by your air of adoration; by the awe with which you listen to his opinions; by the rapt expression on your face when you listen to him monologuing along about himself.

—Dorothy Dix, *How to Win and Hold a Husband*

Some folks might be timid about flirting. They're nervous that they could take things too far, or that they'll flirt inappropriately. Sure, there's a right and a wrong place for flirtation, but personally, I think flirting in the right context is a positive thing: the glances from afar, the "accidental" touch of an arm against an arm, the batting of eyelashes. What courtship ritual is more fun?

*flirt to flatter
the boy*

1963: What about Flirting?

Yes and no. *Yes* if you flirt because you like the boy—or boys in general. *Yes* if you flirt to flatter the boy. *Yes* if you flirt lightly and naturally (girl talking to boy). *Yes* if girls are your friends, too.

No if you flirt only to prove you can make the boy interested. *No* if you plan to drop him the moment he's interested. *No* if you flirt to take him away from a girl who really likes him. *No* if girls think you're bad news to have around.

—Enid A. Haupt, *The Seventeen Book of
Etiquette & Entertaining*

For some instructions to young ladies in the fine art of flirtation with the boy of their dreams (or at least the boy of the evening!), I return now to Ellen Peck's *How to Get a Teen-Age Boy and What to Do with Him When You Get Him* for some excerpts from a chapter on party going.

1969: The Most Serious Flirtation

The most serious flirtation is physical. . . . If it's about time for lights out and you want to be in on the scene, here are a few other things you can do to make sure Neil stays with you instead of taking off in search of Sheila.

Take off something you're wearing. I mean like an *earring*. And toss your hair back and rub your earlobe. Describe the lovely feeling of not having pinched ears any more. Or take off your wristwatch or bracelet and rub your wrist and mention how good *that* feels.

toss your hair back and rub your earlobe

Tell him his shoulders look tense. (He'll think you're fantastically perceptive; but the truth is, it's a safe bet. Nearly always, nearly everybody's shoulders *are* tense.) And that it's important to have relaxed shoulders. And to relax his shoulders he should move them in a circle—forward, then up, then back, then down. You demonstrate this, of course, because when your shoulders are back, your chest looks good.

He, of course, isn't doing it quite right, so you can put your hands on his shoulders to show him how. Then you can tell him his shoulders are not only *tense*, they're *muscular*.

How else physical contact? Touch fingers when he hands you a drink. You shouldn't be smoking, because research says you can *die* from it, but if you are, hold his hand when he lights your cigarette.

When you laugh at something he says, laugh from the torso as you bend over and touch his arm. Or if he's said something serious, you can, wide-eyed, touch his arm as you say, "You don't *mean* it!" You can also touch his arm to signal a change in mood. Like, when you were talking to an unresponsive Neil a few minutes ago, you could have touched his arm lightly as you said, "OK, OK, I'll be serious."

Stand very close. Sit very close. (Not right against him; that's being too obvious.) Look very intensely at him. This is known, in popular parlance, as giving a guy the come-on.

And he nearly always does.

—Ellen Peck, *How to Get a Teen-Age Boy and What to Do with Him When You Get Him*

1969: Party Going

Party behavior is an exaggeration of real behavior. People let themselves go. Flirts become more flirtatious. And, because they get scared by all the action, mice become mousier. Don't be a mouse. Be flirtatious. . . .

Exaggerating things is just one way to be flirtatious. Here's another: be presumptuous. Nervy. Brash. Act like it's just *assumed* that the guy you're talking to admires you a lot more than he really *does*.

You and he both know you're teasing. But amid all the teasing, some ideas can get planted. And, a guy is sure to

ideas can get planted

think a girl with this much self-confidence has something to be confident *about*.

> —Ellen Peck, *How to Get a Teen-Age Boy and What to Do with Him When You Get Him*

While Ellen Peck provides the pro, Mabel Hale gives us the con. You'll need to decide for yourself whom you agree with more.

1922: A Girl's Influence with Boys

Girls have more influence with boys than often they realize. A boy who is rough and rowdy in the presence of one girl will be gentlemanly when with another girl, all because of the girl. If she is "loud" *be reserved and careful* and boisterous, and will laugh at his silly and offensive remarks, he will act on that level; but when he is with a girl who never smiles at that which is rude and vulgar, who is always quiet and modest in her way, he will act as he knows pleases her. He may seem to have the better time with the first girl, but he respects the other girl more. No girl is doing herself justice if she allows the boys any familiarities with her. She can so conduct herself that they will not be taking liberties. Girls should not scuffle with the boys, nor allow them to put their arms about them, to kiss them, nor to hold hands in a silly, sentimental way. Kissing games are foolish and harmful. It is not the proper thing for girls to be seeking, nor too ready to receive, compliments from the boys. Be reserved and careful, and though you do not seem to be so popular as the forward, giddy girl who is always "cutting up" with the boys, you will have the respect of the best boys and young men, and she will not.

—Mabel Hale, *Beautiful Girlhood*

Chapter Six
Looking Good

Q Dear Miss Abigail:

It worked—I snagged him. But I don't have a thing to wear! How should I dress for our first date?

A It's not only how you dress, but how you smell, how your hair is coiffed, how your blush is applied. This chapter will focus on good grooming, an essential part of dating.

This is a perfect time to test your knowledge of a few important topics. The first list of questions is from the home economics book *Everyday Living for Girls*. The test doesn't result in a score, but it does give you the opportunity to reflect upon your personal grooming and to see where improvement is needed.

1936: How Well Are You Groomed?

Following are some questions to be considered in judging whether or not one is well groomed. How many of them can you answer satisfactorily? Talk them over with others in your group and compare opinions. Perhaps you will want to show these questions to your mother or to some older girl or woman and get her opinion as to how well you are groomed. List suggestions of ways by which better grooming can be attained.

Body Cleanliness

1. Do you take a bath or shower every day?
2. Do you use a deodorant?
3. Do you keep the armpits free of hair?
4. Are you free from body odor?
5. If perfume is used, is it fresh, faint, and not cheap?

Face and Neck

1. Is your complexion good, your skin clear?
2. Are your face, neck, and ears clean?
3. Do you use the right shade of powder? Is it entirely invisible?
4. If rouge is used, what principles for selection and use are you trying to follow?
5. What bathing, eating, exercising, and other routines are you following to create an attractive complexion?

Eyebrows and Eyes

1. Are your eyebrows natural and brushed smooth?
2. Are your eyes natural, not exaggerated with make-up?
3. Are your eyes bright, healthy? Do you look straight into the eyes of others as you talk to them?

Hands

1. Are your hands clean?
2. Are they smooth and white, not red and rough?
3. Are your fingers a good color?
4. Are the nails manicured artistically, so that they are pleasing in shape, not too long, too short, too pointed, too square, too vivid, or too shiny?

Hair

1. Does your hair make a becoming frame about your face?
2. Is it tidy?
3. Does it look healthy, alive, well cared for?
4. Is the color natural, not bleached?
5. Is your hair free from dandruff?
6. Do you shampoo it at least once in two weeks?
7. Do you massage your scalp at least once a week?

Teeth and Mouth

1. Are your teeth attractive? That is, do they appear to be in a healthy condition?

is your breath free from bad odors?

2.   Are your lips attractive, soft, not dry and cracked?

3.   Do you promote a good natural color in your lips and cheeks by adequate sleep and exercise, and by medical attention if you are anemic?

4.   Is your breath free from bad odors?

5.   Do you clean your teeth at least twice a day?

6.   Do you have them cleaned by the dentist one or more times a year, or often enough to keep them attractive?

7.   Do you have them regularly examined by the dentist and cared for when needed?

Outer Garments

1.   Are your clothes clean, without spots and odor?

2.   Are they neatly mended where necessary?

3.   If you wear light-colored or white scarfs, collars and cuffs, or flowers, are they clean and neat?

4.   Are your clothes well dressed, without undue wrinkles?

5.   Are they well brushed, without dust, dandruff, and stray hairs? If necessary, do you have a brush in your locker to freshen your garments?

Shoes and Hose

1.   Are your shoes clean and well polished? Do you wipe them off every night? If not, how often? How often do you polish them? Have you a cleaning kit in your room?

2.   Do you keep your heels clean and straight? When you polish shoes, do you polish the backs?

3. Are your hose clean? Do you wear a clean pair of stockings every day? Do you wash your own as most business and college girls do?

4. Do you adjust your stockings straight at the back seam without wrinkles at the ankles?

5. Are they neatly mended, if necessary?

6. Is your hat clean and well brushed?

Accessories

1. Is your jewelry clean?

2. Are your gloves clean?

3. Are they neatly mended, if necessary?

4. Is your purse clean and in good condition?

5. Are your handkerchief, powder puff, and comb clean?

6. Are they kept out of sight?

Undergarments

1. Is your slip the right length for your dress?

are your undergarments clean?

2. Do your shoulder straps show?

3. Are your undergarments clean? That is, do you change them three or four times a week?

—Adelaide Laura Van Duzer, Edna M. Andrix, Ethelwyn L. Bobenmyer, and others, *Everyday Living for Girls*

Now that you've had a chance to determine where you might need improvement, the following excepts should help you improve your grooming skills.

1952: How to Start Using Perfume

Part of a young girl's training in being lovely is the use and care of perfume. A good habit-forming team among her birthday array at about thirteen or fourteen could be her own bottle of toilet water and another, smaller bottle of the same scent, in true perfume. Her toilet water should be complete with atomizer—and a lesson or two—to be sprayed on her hair, her skin, her underthings, and even mixed with the rinse water after her home shampoo.

Her perfume, she will learn, is the accent, used strategically like her lipstick and her jewelry—never loaded on, but always there to be noticed and to attract. And as an accent she will learn to use it lightly and intelligently. She will learn to spray it on, about the face and shoulders, lightly on the hair and on the wrists . . . she will learn the delight of perfume applied to the hem of a dancing dress, to the lining of a coat. Most important of all she will learn the charm and beauty of living graciously, for remembering to surround herself with delicate fragrance is remembering to add pleasure to life.

use it lightly and intelligently

—Nancy Daggett, *Personal Beauty and Charm*

1902: Vegetables Better than Cosmetics

Ladies who wish clear complexions, instead of using cosmetics, eat vegetables and fruit, as long as they are in season; and never throw away cucumber water or the juice of any fruit, but rub your face with it whenever you have it.

eat fruit, girls—good, ripe fruit

Eat fruit, girls—good, ripe fruit, however—if you would have and keep a clear and beautiful skin.

Practice smiles, also, not frowns. There is a wonderful charm in a smile. Like charity, it hides a multitude of sins.

—Professor B. G. Jefferis, *The Household Guide, or Domestic Cyclopedia*

1963: Makeup

A young woman of refinement will never be conspicuous because of the misuse or overuse of all that is sold at a cosmetic counter. She will wear very little makeup in the classroom, perhaps nothing more than lipstick or powder. She knows that stage makeup is for the stage and not for the street. She knows, too, that the type of boy she would like to interest is not impressed by excess makeup, but more often he is revolted by it. Your own brother is the man to verify this statement.

I asked one student body of four hundred composed of all boys at a prep school on the West Coast what they disliked most about girls. The answer of the greater number can be summarized in the answer of one boy: "Too much of that junk on their face!" Interestingly enough, I did not see one young man in that group who dressed in a bizarre fashion. Somehow I feel if one had been present, he would have said, "I like it!" He is the type of boy who usually seeks out the girl who, like himself, likes lots and lots of it.

too much of that junk on their face!

—Anne Culkin, *Charm for Young Women*

1904: Care of the Hair

Feminine loveliness and fascination still find one of their chief aids in the ample growth and graceful arrangement of the hair, and so few, indeed, are the women who to save a little trouble would willingly sacrifice this beauty by wearing the hair clipped short, that they are nearly apt to be considered lacking in true feminine instinct. Nearly all women are willing to give to this part of the person the required care, for the sake of the resulting pleasure afforded themselves and others. . . .

Use of the Curling Iron

As to the curling iron it has ruined many beautiful heads of hair. If the iron is used carefully and at the proper heat the hair is not injured, but if the iron is too hot it burns the life out of the hair and its brilliancy is gone. If the curling iron is too hot, stop using it or wrap soft paper around it.

Brushing

A good hair-brush, or two of them, skill- *twenty-five to* fully and regularly used, will prove the best *fifty strokes* of tonics for hair and scalp. All tangles should first be removed with the comb. Taking the brush, apply it first with a short, circular, scrubbing motion, to every portion of the scalp;

not vigorously enough to cause soreness, but just enough to penetrate the hair and enliven the circulation of the blood, thus stimulating the oil glands. The brush is then applied to the hair itself, from roots to ends, with firm, gentle, even strokes. Twenty-five to fifty strokes, given night and morning, will keep the hair beautifully soft and glossy, and is better than any pomade which could be used.

—Mary Ries Melendy, *Vivilore: The Pathway to Mental and Physical Perfection*

This next quiz will help you determine whether your choice of clothing is fashionable or faddish. I'm sure you can look back upon your wardrobe choices over the years and see more fad than fashion (remember the eighties?). Let's try not to make the same mistakes again, particularly on that first date!

1969: Fashion or Fad?

What is a fad, and how does it differ from a fashion?
A fad, your dictionary will tell you, is a "temporary," usually "irrational" pursuit which
"excites attention." While fashion is
national, even worldwide in scope, a fad is
usually confined to a small group, a town, or
a geographical section.

a fad is attention-getting

A fad is temporary, while a fashion lasts at least a season—often longer.

A fad is attention-getting, while true fashion abhors the conspicuous.

Fads can be fun, or, by their extreme nature, they can be so unsightly as to be painful to the beholder. Such fads are usually in the sloppy category. Other fads are so objectionable or harmful that they are actually taboo.

Can You Tell the Difference?

Here is a list of recent fads. Indicate those you think are *Fun* and harmless (F), *Sloppy* and unsightly (S), objectionable and *Taboo* (T).

1. You wear nonprescription, rimless granny glasses. ____
2. You wear your skirts a couple of inches below the knee when everyone else shows several inches of thigh. ____
3. You wear knee socks with date dresses. ____
4. You wear a long thrift shop dress to a party when everyone else is in short, shiny dresses. ____
5. You never have your hair trimmed, because you're proud of its length. ____

6. You paste decals on your legs. ___

7. You wear a sweater so skin-tight that it shows the outline of your bra. ___

8. You wear an army jacket to school. ___

9. You wear a scarf tied above your knee. ___

10. You wear a ring on every finger. ___

11. You wear the shortest of micro skirts, even though you're over a size fourteen. ___

12. You wear black tights with stiletto-heeled shoes. ___

13. You wear stretch pants so tight that the outline of your panty girdle shows. ___

14. You wear slogan buttons that are apt to offend minority groups. ___

15. You wear a leather band around your forehead, Indian fashion. ___

16. You wear as many bead necklaces as you can bear. ___

17. You wear black lacy tights to school. ___

18. You wear "his" turtleneck to school, although it's several sizes too large. ___

19. You wear half a dozen chains, plus keys about your waist as a belt. ___

20. You wear your skirts so short that the tops of your stockings show. ___

Answers: F for 1, 6, 8, 10, 15, 16, 19; S for 3, 5, 11, 18, 20; T for 2, 4, 7, 9, 12, 13, 14, 17. Give yourself 5 points for each correct answer. A score of 100 means you know a fad from a fashion; 80 or more signifies you're human after all; 60 to 80 suggests that you're either too proper or too sloppy in your dress; under 60 is an invitation to try again.

—Kay Thomas, *Secrets of Loveliness*

Uh-oh. I got a score of 55. I hope you did better than I did!

1963: Dress for the Occasion

One of a girl's greatest assets is femininity. Do not sacrifice it. Enjoy dressing for the party or the social occasion. Casual dress does not mean sloppy dress. Boys can wear shorts and slacks, but remember they would look a little ridiculous in a dress. So you wear what he cannot wear as often as you can. Did you ever notice how different you act when you are all dressed up? You rise to the occasion, don't you? Boys do the same thing. Your dressing up is one way of trying to inspire him to do the same.

—Anne Culkin, *Charm for Young Women*

Quizzes and scores aside, it's important to note that despite all you do with your hair, makeup, perfume, clean underwear, and great-looking clothes, you won't make a desirable impression on your date without a charming personality. Remember what you learned in chapter 3? Author Catherine Atkinson Miller reminds us of the importance of personality in the following:

1933: Personality Counts More than Appearance

Nothing is more disappointing than meeting a delightful-looking young woman and discovering that her personality is no more vivid than that of a rag doll. Pretty clothes can be bought ready-made but you must make your own personality—that total expression of you which is the result of your characteristic attitudes, thoughts, and actions. Some people's attitudes toward life are so negative, their thoughts so commonplace, and their actions so obvious that we may speak of them as lacking personality. We mean, actually, that they lack the kind of personality which most people like—a vivid, attractive, wholesome personality.

You must make your own personality but you cannot do it directly, as you would make a cake, stating, "Now I shall make a cake," and then carefully following the routine of measuring, mixing, baking, frosting, and so achieving a luscious result which will disappear as

vivid, attractive, wholesome personality

soon as the family discovers it. If you should declare, "Now I shall develop a charming personality," and concentrate all your attention on doing so, you would become a conceited prig and repel the very persons you most desired to attract. Curiously enough, *you develop personality most effectively by forgetting all about it!*

Just as happiness usually comes when you are so busy doing something for someone else that you forget to look for it, so does personality develop quietly and surely as you live a busy, wholesome life filled with eager awareness of other people and of all the thrilling things which make the world, and life, so exciting. . . .

The strength and charm of your personality depend upon the degree to which you are able to live fully; enjoying natural and man-made beauty, finding new ideas and dreams in books, proving yourself in stimulating work, relating yourself to the problems of your time, forgetting yourself in happy relationships with other people.

—Catherine Atkinson Miller, *Eighteen: The Art of Being a Woman*

1911: Masculine Attention

No woman is entitled to any more attention than her loveliness and ladylike conduct will command. Those who are most pleasing will receive the most attention, and those who desire more should aspire to acquire more by cultivating those graces and virtues which ennoble woman, but no lady should lower or distort her own true ideal, or smother and crucify her conscience, in order to please any living man. A good man will admire a good woman, and deceptions cannot long be concealed. Her show of dry goods or glitter of jewels cannot long cover up her imperfections or deceptions.

—Professor B. G. Jefferis and J. L. Nichols, *Search Lights on Health: Light on Dark Corners: A Complete Sexual Science and a Guide to Purity and Physical Manhood, Advice to Maiden, Wife and Mother, Love, Courtship and Marriage*

Chapter Seven
You're Dating!

Q Dear Miss Abigail:
I made the call, and she accepted my offer of a date. What are some basics I should be aware of?

A Before you even think about walking up the steps of your date's house (you are picking her up, aren't you?), I want to make sure that you know how to best present yourself on your big night out. Not to her, silly—to her *family!*

1943: Meeting the Parents

To date expertly is a matter of solving a few initial problems. There's the sleuthing to discover what will meet with the girl and her family's approval. There's sales promotion, for girls date more easily if they know that a boy has a fascinating personality, strong character, and an aptitude for choosing the right associations. Then there's the approach: invitations worded so definitely and so persuasively that they inspire "Yes"s. . . .

To avoid disappointment the wise boy dates early. How far ahead is determined by the nature of the date. If made considerably in advance, as for a formal party, the boy gives her a reminder. He then tells her the hour that he will call, the mode of transportation, the personnel of the group, and, if sending a corsage, asks the color of her dress. This last-minute checkup eliminates mistakes.

The big night arrives. The boy rings the doorbell on time. When admitted to the house, he introduces himself quietly and confidently. He stands until the ladies present are seated. This constitutes the first social hurdle. He undoubtedly would have preferred to give curb service, but how could he impress the family favorably with a honk?

Once seated in the living room he converses actively on the subject of her dad's golf score and her mother's bridge. To gain his entree, he did the sleuthing. He knows this interest in their hobbies is politic.

he did the sleuthing

The lady floats in—not too tardily. He rises and assists her with her wraps. They speak a pleasant "good night" to the parents, and perhaps suggest casually the hour of return. He allows her to precede him as they leave. All this gentlemanly behavior has undoubtedly won the family's heart.

—M. Thelma McAndless, *Manners Today*

1939: The Boy You Like

Not only do you let a boy know by words that you like him. Your actions and your consideration of him are revealing. You graciously accept his invitations—"Yes, I'd like to go. Thank you for asking me." You do not take it as a matter of fact that on Saturday night he will provide entertainment for you. You are ready when he calls for you. When you are with him, you let him know that the evening is enjoyable—"It's a good picture, isn't it?" or, "I'm glad we came to the party." You act as though you were proud of him; you introduce him to your friends; you create opportunities for him to display to advantage whatever talents he has; you talk with him as though his conversation really interested you. Nothing more quickly blasts a friendship than a matter-of-course attitude, rudeness, or lack of sincerity; accepting invitations and gifts as though they were your due; being bored or looking around for other conquests during a boy's conversation; leaving him flat for several dances because you have found a better dancer; "handing him a line" but not meaning what you say.

—Ruth Fedder, *A Girl Grows Up*

act as though you were proud of him

You may be wondering just how often you should be taking girls out on dates. Whether you two are steady or not-quite-steady, this, from none other than game show host Allen Ludden, should help answer your questions.

1954: How Many Dates Make a Week?

The generally accepted pattern for steady couples in high school is one midweek evening date with a comparatively early curfew, Friday and Saturday nights, and Sunday afternoon. That's a grand total of four dates a week without any "unbearable" spans of time in between, and it's a pretty tough schedule to maintain at that. Unless you're convinced that your personal charm is indefatigable, you'll be wise not to exceed that four-date limit. After all, there's quite a bit to be said for the "absence makes the heart grow fonder" routine. And, no matter how woefully the Little Lady seems to be smitten, she's apt to become a sorry kitten rather quickly if she discovers your tent pitched on her doorstep. She'll tire of you and start treating you like that doorstop in incredibly short order! Women are like that.

a footloose and fancy-free young swain

If you're going steady, plan a reasonable schedule together and stick to it. If you're not going steady, relax. The "four-date" business isn't for you. Since you'll be dating far less frequently than your enslaved brothers, you'll be able to put more planning and—let's face it, money—into each social whirl. As a footloose and fancy-free young swain, you'll just step out when you're sufficiently moved. Whatever you do, don't get the idea you're a social misfit if you wind up spending a Saturday night with the boys now and then. It can be a refreshing change, and that's often the topic of conversation "when good fellows get together!"

—Allen Ludden, *Plain Talk! For Men Under 21!*

1939: "Don'ts" Every Girl Should Know

DON'T look overjoyed when a man dates you up. Take it as a matter of course. A man thinks he must be a sap if he is the only one who ever notices you. Act as if you could take 'em or leave 'em and it didn't matter which to you.

DON'T be too easy. No man wants the peach that threatens to fall in his mouth whether he desires it or not. The one he craves is the one that he has to climb a little for, but not too much nor too high. So calculate your distance and don't really get beyond arm's reach.

DON'T make your flattery too obvious. All men are vain and like to be complimented, but they want it done artistically.

DON'T accept *every* invitation a boy offers you. Stay at home now and then. The harder it is to get a date with a girl, the more eager a boy is for it. Men always want some other man's OK on a woman.

DON'T think that you can get by with just a pretty face. That's all to the good, of course, but if a girl wants to make a hit with men she has to have a lot of parlor tricks besides. She has to know how to be entertaining and amusing; how to dance and play a good game of bridge; how to fit in any company.

she has to have a lot of parlor tricks

—Dorothy Dix, *How to Win and Hold a Husband*

We can't be reminded too often of what constitutes proper behavior in the company of others. Here are some helpful tips on this matter, for guys and girls alike.

1940: Private Affairs

While care of the person is an important matter, it is not one to be attended to in the presence of witnesses. A boy cleaning and filing his nails in public is as unalluring a sight as one washing his neck and ears or brushing his teeth. A girl who combs her hair or goes through makeup contortions under public gaze loses some of her charm. The majority of men feel a certain disgust watching such actions. A dressing room, bedroom, or bathroom is the place for you to make the toilet. If, when you are out, you can inconspicuously run a clean powder puff over your face, no one will accuse you of indelicacy. But even this is unbecoming when you do it repeatedly, for it suggests far too much thought of your person and not enough thought of your companions. What would you think of a man who, while with you in a restaurant, whisked out an electric razor, plugged it into a wall socket, produced a pocket mirror, and shaved himself?

Here is the rule to go by. Do nothing in company that calls attention to the body or its functions. Stifle a yawn you feel coming on, if you can; if you cannot, at least cover your gaping mouth. If and when you must blow your nose, get out your handkerchief inconspicuously and do it as quietly as possible without making the act

avoid in any company

more noticeable by apologizing for it, unless you have had to stop in the midst of speaking. Follow the same practice when you are forced to sneeze or cough. Throat-clearing, scratching, cleaning out the ears, picking the teeth, spitting, and similar unpleasant acts all well-bred people avoid in any company.

—Eleanor Boykin, *This Way, Please: A Book of Manners*

I'm aware that so far I've focused quite a bit in this book on how young women are expected to act and look on their dates. I certainly don't want to leave anyone out, so I've pulled together a few excerpts geared toward the men in the audience to end this chapter. Enjoy!

1954: The Masculine Angle

Good grooming, courtesy, and a pleasant personality are the qualities that girls rate as most important in their dates. A boy is considered courteous if he does the many little things that make a girl feel well taken care of: devoting himself to her rather than to some other girl in the crowd; helping her with her coat; opening doors for her; letting her precede him unless his leading the way will make it easier for her (when going up and down dark or treacherous stairs, through crowds, along paths with low-hanging branches, getting out of vehicles); sitting and walking on her left whenever possible; choosing movies where they need not stand long in line; giving her order in restaurants; and behaving maturely and with poise in all times and places.

behaving maturely and with poise

Although a boy should never expect his girl to "go Dutch" on a date, there are occasions when sharing the expenses seems fair and natural. He should borrow money from her only in an emergency and then repay her promptly. Although he need not hesitate to add up a bill, he will embarrass his date if he quarrels with the cashier over a minor check error. The courtesy he shows to waitresses, cab drivers, and filling-station attendants is a definite indication of his character.

A boy who tells off-color stories, makes offensive remarks, or criticizes a girl in front of others or behind her back will soon find it difficult to make dates with well-bred girls.

—Mary Beery, *Manners Made Easy*

1911: Dress Affects Our Manners

A man who is badly dressed feels chilly, sweaty, and prickly. He stammers, and does not always tell the truth. He means to, perhaps, but he can't. He is half distracted about his pantaloons, which are much too short, and are constantly hitching up; or his frayed jacket and crumpled linen harrow his soul, and quite unman him.

half distracted about his pantaloons

—Professor B. G. Jefferis and J. L. Nichols, *Search Lights on Health: Light on Dark Corners: A Complete Sexual Science and a Guide to Purity and Physical Manhood, Advice to Maiden, Wife and Mother, Love, Courtship and Marriage*

Chapter Eight

What to Do on a Date

Q   Dear Miss Abigail:
Our date is set, but we haven't made specific plans yet. What sort of fun activities do you suggest?

A   Now is when things really start to get exciting. The possibilities are endless: movies, theater, dinner, dancing, long walks on the beach at sunset—okay, okay, I'm sounding too much like a personals ad. The point is, your date can be anything the two of you want it to be. This chapter offers up some guidance on what types of things might be appropriate for your date.

1943: **What to Do on a Date**

For a movie date the lady decides upon the picture. Afterward she's likely to expect a hot fudge. If her appetite tends to be more extravagant, the boy is privileged to stake out boundaries.

Boys and girls do better in the dating business if they have cultivated a variety of interests. If one can sing, dance, bowl, and swim, he's fourfold fortunate. The versatile individual finds a pleasant date for every mood.

a pleasant date for every mood

Dates are not necessarily the boy's responsibility; the girls in very subtle ways manage many of them. The smooth feminine approach is to plan friendly get-togethers such as hikes, bicycle jaunts, wiener roasts. The object of their affection discovers how charming, how intelligent, how clever is the modern girl. He learns, too, that the girl he wants to know better is tactful and considerate; that she makes an effort to understand him, and that she compliments skillfully. Then, even if she's not beautiful, she is likely to look good to him.

—M. Thelma McAndless, *Manners Today.*

1956: Let the Girl Know Where

The boy should also be careful to let the girl know where they are to go on the date. It's no fun for either if he arrives in sports clothes with a wiener bake in mind, and finds his date dressed in her Sunday best.

with a wiener bake in mind

—Clyde M. Narramore, *Life and Love: A Christian View of Sex*

Sometime in your dating life, you're sure to end up at the prom or at another formal dance. And in terms of classic advice, dancing is quite the hot topic. Authors in every era have had opinions about whether you should or should not attend dances, and, if you do, how you should behave while there. But don't forget—the prom is just like any other day (on which you dress up in a frilly dress and wear flowers pinned to your shoulder and get your photo taken in front of a goofy canopy!), so don't sweat it. You'll do just fine.

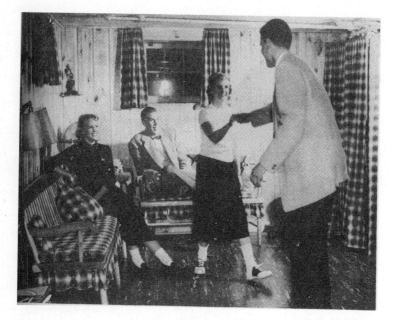

1923: May I Have This Dance?

If a girl accepts a boy's invitation to a dance, the boy arranges to call for his companion at her home and, of course, acts as her escort both to and from the affair. If a definite time for starting has been agreed upon, it is a matter of courtesy for a girl to be ready on time. When the girl is very young, or when her parents are notably particular, it

they may harmonize with her dress

is polite for her escort to ascertain the time at which her parents wish her to reach home. If the boy's finances permit, he may provide flowers for the girl, in which case he often consults her preference so that they may harmonize with her dress. It is customary for an escort to claim the first and last dances as well as the dance just preceding and the one following the intermission. He sees that the girl has partners for the various numbers—also, when refreshments are in order, that she is served. He assumes the responsibility for her enjoyment. The boys whose names appear on her program, or others whom she may know, or to whom she may be introduced, ask, "May I have this dance?" She answers graciously, "Yes, you may," or "I think you may," or "I'm sorry, but this dance is taken." At the end of the dance, it is the boy's place to express the pleasure the dance has afforded him. His partner replies, "I am glad you enjoyed it," or "I enjoyed it, too." Both boys and girls should be careful to dance in such a way as to avoid giving the impression that they do not come from homes of refinement.

—Faculty of the South Philadelphia High School for Girls,
Everyday Manners for American Boys and Girls

Although the following author's perspective is a bit extreme, cautious girls might take his concerns into consideration when deciding whether or not to accept an invitation to a dance.

1838: Ball Fatigue

We often fatigue and unfit ourselves for mental efforts, and destroy, for the time, our moral energies, by the exciting nature of our amusements. A young lady is often so

her moral energies are prostrated

engrossed in the anticipations of a ball or assembly, so absorbed in thought and feeling while preparing for it, and so highly excited amidst its scenes, that she is unfitted for any vigorous and profitable intellectual efforts for days after. And, then too, in the fatigue which follows, her moral energies are prostrated. Had this young lady simply danced at home, with her brothers and sisters, or with friends and neighbors who might be present, without any previous feverish anticipations, or any fatiguing preparations, it would have been a healthful and refreshing amusement.

—Jason Whitman, *The Young Lady's Aid,*
to Usefulness and Happiness

Dances, according to some, can be downright evil events—something that young ladies should stay away from . . . if they want to protect their virginity!

1938: The Devil's Invention

Perfect dancing, as all dancers will readily admit, demands perfect movement; that is, the two bodies must move as one. To this end the bodies are locked together by one arm placed about a woman's waist as they stand facing each other, with one of the woman's hands resting upon the man's shoulder; her heaving breasts are against his while her right hand is held in his left; he places his foot between hers. To begin with, this position may be effected by the bodies being kept somewhat apart, but almost irresistibly the bodies come more and more in contact, mingling the sexes in such closeness of personal approach and contact as, outside the dance, is nowhere tolerated in respectable society. To this must be added, the young woman is improperly attired with a sleeveless, low-necked dress exposing more or less of her secondary sexual charms, her breasts. From this description any reasonable person can easily see that the modern dance has been contrived by evil minds but for one purpose, and that to awaken and arouse the sex nature, and to give human passions leave to disport themselves unreproved by conscience or reason, almost at will.

Now let us consider for a moment what this means. It is evening, the hour is late, the room is crowded, there is the intoxication of sensual jazz music which is intended to arouse the baser passions of both men and women. The women are *this giddy whirl goes on* dressed so as to set off their sexual charms, they are exposed to hot and poisoned air, perspiring bodies in close embrace, the personal electricity passing between the clasped hands, the hot breath of the man blown upon the exposed chest and arms of the woman; and still, hour after hour this giddy whirl goes on until the dancers have covered a distance of from twelve to fifteen miles in an average evening's dance. Oh, the horrors of it all! Could the devil have possibly conceived of anything more diabolical than his invention of the modern dance?

—Oscar Lowry, *A Virtuous Woman: Sex Life in Relation to the Christian Life*

After writing *A Virtuous Woman: Sex Life in Relation to the Christian Life* in 1938, author Oscar Lowry wrote a book for the other sex in 1940: *The Way of a Man with a Maid: Sexology for Men and Boys.* These books provide an interesting contrast, and the titles alone have afforded me much amusement. I mean, how's a girl supposed to remain virtuous with all those boys and men out there scheming to have their way with her?

What if your date suggests doing something that you find, shall we say, less than desirable? What if the boy has a fancy car and would like to take the girl to a roadhouse—and this is his only idea? No matter how tempting that might sound, it might be better to suggest something else to do on your date (or to date someone else entirely!). Young ladies may want to heed the advice of Elinor Glyn. Please, for the sake of your virginity!

1925: Joy-riding to the Roadhouse

In some respects, the automobile has become a disturbing element in the lives of boys and girls. In years past, courtship progressed at the girl's home, on lovers'-lane strolls, at parties, dances, and the like, while today the automobile and good roads enable the young people quickly to reach comparatively distant points of entertainment. Roadhouses and wayside inns have sprung up at places of necessary and desirable remoteness, where the restraints of nearby residents are not available for quelling unruly emotions and passions that follow coarse music and inferior liquor. So, young girls, unless you have been reared with a happy sense of restraint and the fitness of things, you endanger your peace of mind and your good repute by frequenting roadhouses in the company of casual male companions.

coarse music and inferior liquor

True it is that parents are much to blame for a certain slackness in the training and observation of their children. Father and mother, with their car, cannot always expect daughter and her friend to be satisfied to motor quietly about with them. If the parents are too often joyriding alone themselves, they can hardly expect daughter to remain at home looking over the latest styles or trying out the newest fox-trot.

—Elinor Glyn, *This Passion Called Love*

With all this talk of all the craziness out there at roadhouses and dances, I wouldn't blame you if you decided to simply make an evening of it at home with your friends.

1961: Dates at Home

For honest-to-goodness, inexpensive fun, how about dates at home with a group of your friends, where you, in cooperation with your parents, provide the entertainment and amusements? Roll back the rugs; put a stack of your favorite records on the phonograph; and the party will be set for hours. Everyone enjoys home-baked cakes or cookies and the fun of making his or her own special brand of sandwich. You know what fun it is to gather around a piano and sing—just for your own pleasure and delight. You know it, too: you'd rather be doing things yourselves than watching some movie or stage show. You're the happiest when dancing, singing, or playing challenging games.

everyone enjoys home-baked cakes

Amid such carefree fun, the boys and girls around you show their true characters and temperaments. By observing them you can start deciding what qualities you will someday seek in a life partner. Your teen years are precious; much is to be learned from staying with the group.

—"A Friend of Youth." *20th-Century Teenagers*

Dinner dates are another popular way to get to know someone. But an evening at a restaurant can also be a crucial (and sometimes scary) test of your manners. Follow these rules and you'll impress the heck out of your companion. I promise.

1880: General Rules for Behavior at Table

- Tea and coffee should never be poured into a saucer.

keep your elbows at your side

- If a person wishes to be served with more tea or coffee, he should place his spoon in the saucer. If he has had sufficient, let it remain in the cup.
- If anything unpleasant is found in the food, such as a hair in the bread or a fly in the coffee, remove it without remark. Though your own appetite be spoiled, it is well not to spoil that of others.
- Never, if possible, cough or sneeze at the table. If you feel the paroxysm coming on, leave the room. It may be worthwhile to know that a sneeze may be stifled by placing the finger firmly upon the upper lip.
- Fold your napkin when you are done with it and place it in your ring, when at home. If you are visiting, leave your napkin unfolded beside your plate.
- Never hold your knife and fork upright on each side of your plate while you are talking.
- Do not cross your knife and fork upon your plate until you have finished.
- When you send your plate to be refilled, place your knife and fork upon one side of it or put them upon your piece of bread.

- Eat neither too fast nor too slow.
- Never lean back in your chair nor sit too near or too far from the table.
- Keep your elbows at your side, so that you may not inconvenience your neighbors.
- Do not find fault with the food.
- The old-fashioned habit of abstaining from taking the last piece upon the plate is no longer observed. It is to be supposed that the vacancy can be supplied if necessary.
- If a plate is handed you at table, keep it yourself instead of passing it to a neighbor. If a dish is passed to you, serve yourself first, then pass it.

> —John A. Ruth, *Decorum: A Practical Treatise on Etiquette and Dress of the Best American Society*

1950: Odoriferous Food

I once heard a young man say, "I should care whether my girlfriend likes onions or not. If I want to eat onions, I eat them. If she doesn't like it, she knows what she can do."

its odor may disturb others

Such a person is the personification of selfishness. The poor girl may be helpless. She has no other boyfriend at the present time, and is forced to go out with Jack, who chooses to eat onions that evening. No one wants to be accused of having halitosis. Eating onions is courting a form of halitosis which is really more objectionable than the unavoidable kind, because the implied discourtesy irritates.

It is discourteous to order at a restaurant any food which through its odor may disturb others at table. Such foods are strong cheese, onions, chives, garlic.

It is inconsiderate for the same reason to eat oranges, bananas, and certain other foods on trains or boats around neighboring passengers who may be ill by their odor.

—Sophie C. Hadida, *Manners for Millions*

You may be wondering what you're supposed to talk about while you're on your date. Need we say that it's important to be able to carry on a conversation with someone you are spending a lot of time with, whether for a few dates or a lifetime commitment? Imagine years of staring at each other across the table with nothing to say! Better brush up on those conversation skills and carry your weight, all the while looking out for someone who matches your pace.

1907: Conversation: Manner

Let us consider manner in conversation, which is as important as the subject matter.

flippancy grates upon one's nerves

First, interest is essential. You must be in earnest. Interest in your subject inspires fitting expression of your thought. When heartiness is lacking, when a person talks without enthusiasm, the listener soon becomes "bored."

Persons, too, who are never serious are very tiresome. Flippancy grates upon one's nerves if long continued.

Nervousness in talking is often a matter of health, and shyness is exaggerated humility.

Concentrate your attention upon what you are saying, not upon how you are saying it.

Self-respect is neither humble nor arrogant.

Hesitations, mannerisms, coughing when at a loss for a word, are forms of nervousness that a little self-will exerted in the right direction may easily control.

Don't make grimaces or assume an artificial sparkle. Let interest in your subject give animation to your face.

A sympathetic manner is very winning—feeling with others and in the direction of their thought. It implies a disposition to wish to agree, at least, rather than to differ from and oppose what another says.

No one likes a mere echo of his sentiments and opinions, however. Bishop Huntington says: "It is a mistake to imagine that we always please people by agreeing with them. One's own deliberate conviction, modestly and courteously spoken, is a generous contribution to the public intellectual wealth."

Not less unpleasant than the meekly acquiescent talkers are the aggressive ones who lay down the law and will permit no one to disagree with them without an agreement. Disputatious persons ought to be muzzled.

—New York Society of Self-Culture, *Correct Social Usage.*

After you process all that advice, let's hope you are not coming across as dull. That would be terribly detrimental to a relationship.

1929: Dullness Is Out

But suppose you are dull? You know it, but oh, how you would like to have personality, lots of friends, your opinion sought after!

minds respond to exercise

The answer is that you can't, and continue to be stupid and dull. You can have personality, though, if you start at the root of things and consciously and intellectually develop your mind and your interests.

Minds respond to exercise just as do any other muscles in the body.

But a little exercise today, none tomorrow, and a little some other time, is worse than useless.

Reading novels and seeing movies do not in themselves constitute mental exercise. Both of them can be mental exercise, though, if you use them to provoke analytical thought.

—Daré Frances, *Lovely Ladies: The Art of Being a Woman*

E-mail correspondence, a staple of modern dating life, is obviously not touched upon in classic advice, since the Internet wasn't around back then. Now, I know that it is a convenient method of correspondence, but it is my duty to remind you that e-mail is not quite as romantic as a *handwritten* note or letter, if romance is your goal (I discuss this a bit more in chapter 14, when we delve further into expressions of love). Whatever your method of transmission, I beg of you to maintain courtesy in writing, and to mind your p's and q's—not to mention running spell-check every now and again when sending messages electronically. As this brief passage reminds us, some things never change.

1927: Social Correspondence

Social correspondence assumes added importance as our lives grow busier. Now that the visits of a generation ago which lasted the better part of an afternoon *be gracious as well* are superseded by a moment's stop in a motor and the dropping of cards; when a note must ofttimes accomplish as much as a lengthy call; it behooves us not only to be correct in our correspondence, but to be gracious as well.

—Eaton, Crane & Pike Company, *A Desk Book on the Etiquette of Letter Writing and Social Correspondence in General*

You've gone to dinner with the girl of your dreams; you've watched the summer blockbuster at your local movie theater. Now it's the end of the evening and time to drop your date off at home, and you're feeling unprepared for what comes next—the good-night kiss!

1958: Rules for a Beginner

Kissing is not a game. Believe me! It means a lot more than just a pleasant pastime, a forfeit, or a test of popularity. I can tell you for sure that if you get to thinking of it that way, you're dead wrong. A kiss is a beautiful expression of love—real love. Not only that, it is a powerful stimulus of emotion. Kissing for fun is like

kissing is not a game

playing with a beautiful candle in a roomful of dynamite! And it's like

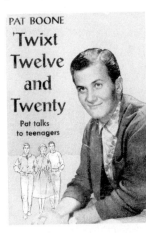

any other beautiful thing—when it ceases to be rare, it loses its value and much of its beauty. I really think it's better to amuse ourselves in some other way. For your own future enjoyment I say go bowling, or to a basketball game, or watch a good TV program (like the *Pat Boone Chevy* show!), at least for a while. Take it easy. Keep to the middle course. No extremes.

—Pat Boone, *'Twixt Twelve and Twenty*
Pat Talks to Teenagers

1916: Natural Sentiments of Boys and Girls

It is natural for a girl to shrink from the touch of a boy's arm about her person and to resent every attempt on the part of a boy to kiss her. It is just as natural for the well-trained boy to be chivalrous toward girls. This sense of modesty and discretion on the part of a girl and the feeling of tenderness and protection on the part of the boy can be easily overcome by a social atmosphere that approves of hugging and kissing. Many erring girls can trace their step toward ruin to a kiss in childhood. Many men can trace their conquest of women to their boyish exploits in kissing small girls.

When home training and teaching become sane and natural, boys and girls will come to maturity with unkissed lips, friendship will deepen naturally into intelligent pure love, courtship will terminate in happy marriage, and divorce cases will disappear from our court dockets.

—Professor T. W. Shannon, *Nature's Secrets Revealed: Scientific Knowledge of the Laws of Sex Life and Heredity, or Eugenics*

Some may find the "aftertaste" of one kiss not as enjoyable as the aftertaste of another. For those with concerns about the aftereffects of smooching, here's some guidance as to those feelings you may have the morning after locking lips.

1948: Aftertaste?

Some young people report having tried relationships once or twice and

finding that they had a sort of "dark brown taste" the next
morning. They had a slight revulsion of feeling; they
wished they hadn't done it. In all honesty they   *as beautiful*
could say when a similar situation arose,   *as the faraway*
"Nothing doing; I don't like the aftereffects."   *music of a*
Others, under other circumstances, have found   *violin*
that after a blissful comradeship, after the fun of talk
together and play together and work together, that the lingering
good-night which brought hands and perhaps lips together, made a fitting ending. It became for them, as they thought back upon it, as beautiful as the faraway music of a violin over a lake at sunset time. They
found it sheer beauty. The feeling which the experience leaves is not the
only consideration but it should be honestly taken into account.

    —Grace Loucks Elliott and Harry Bone, *The Sex Life of Youth*

1972: There's More to Your Mouth

A voluptuous mouth is a mouth that is carefully and definitely
outlined with a brush or pencil—the outline must be darker than
the lip color. If your lips are thin, be sure to powder your lips first
and go slightly above the outline. If your lips are full, go ever so
slightly *under* your own lip line. Now fill in with lipstick. Check
with whomever you're trying to please to see which shades of lipstick he likes on you. Then take a brush and paint gloss over your
lips. The lips have little or no oil or moisture in them and have a
tendency to look or be dry. The gloss that you apply is not only
beneficial—it's what gives that sensuous look to the lips.

    Look in the mirror, say the word "True," hold the position with

your lips. . . . Don't be afraid to practice a few tempting movements of your lips. You'll find they become natural to you—and
the reaction to those lips is going to be spontaneous combustion.

—Eileen Ford, *Eileen Ford's A More Beautiful You in 21 Days*

1932: Kissing

A kiss is not just a touch of the lips—there must be warmth and tenderness that convey the thought back of the lips to make it a clinging
caress, a desire to return for more—just as the bee returns to the
blossom. This is what must be found in the love union to make it sweet
and beautiful, for it is just as truly a kiss of more intense warmth and
tenderness—an infinitely more clinging caress.

There is as much difference between kisses as
between light and darkness. Some men and women
are natural-born kissers; and there are others that
could not excel if they should live to be a thousand

*a blending,
melting
softness*

years old. Kissing itself is an art, and it takes experience to be a good kisser. Some women just "peck" in their kissing. Some women draw their lips tightly over the teeth, indicating too much rigidity, particularly in a woman with thin lips. Naturally, full, rounded lips furnish the most alluring, intriguing mouth for a kiss, but, in any event, whether the lips are full or thin, in kissing for the real pleasure of the act, the mouth should be held softly, with lips curled slightly out, with teeth slightly separated. The man should put his lips to those of his partner with a blending, melting softness. Avoid overly moist kisses; they are not esthetic.

—Frederick M. Rossiter, *The Torch of Life: A Key to Sex Harmony*

The kissing advice is great, but what if you are having difficulty getting your guy to lean in for that smooch in the first place? Take note, ladies: Barbara Lang has a few ideas about what to do in this case.

1965: Yes, Please

Once in a great while, you might want your date to kiss you good night even though the idea has not occurred to him. Now if there is a paucity of literature on how exactly to *avoid* being kissed good night, there is not a word anywhere on just what you can do to *get* kissed. In fact, the only people who will tackle the question at all are the soap, deodorant, and mouthwash companies, and their approach is really rather a negative one. It's also pretty eerie. If I ever saw my romance fade, fade, fade away and dissolve into thin air, I wouldn't reach for a toothpaste, I'd apply for the booby hatch.

But to go back to the problem of what to do on those rare occasions when you would like your date to kiss you good night. The people who know how apparently aren't talking. The most you get from them is a suggestion that you lean toward him and look up expectantly. I did that once and my date offered me a cigarette. A dreamy, yearning look is apt to provoke a comment such as, "You OK?" or "Hey, do you wear contact lenses?"

I can think of only one thing to suggest, and I can't tell you why it has worked once or twice for me. The thing to do is to look at his lips—not from across the room, but standing fairly close to him. This seems to remind him that they're there and *keep looking at his lips* may provoke him into touching them to yours. On the other hand, a self-conscious boy is apt to take out a handkerchief because he guesses he has mustard on his mouth from the hot dog he ate at the game. Even if he does that, keep looking at his lips. He may still give in and kiss you. (On the other hand, he may break out in fever sores.)

That's really the only slightly subtle approach I can suggest for this problem. There are of course other more obvious moves you can make. You might, for example, ask him, "Do you like this perfume?" and then collapse against him so he can smell your neck. Be prepared for him to wrinkle up his nose and reply that it smells like A-1 Sauce. Boys are not too bright at times like this. At least mine never have been, but I wish you the very best of luck.

—Barbara Lang, *Boys and Other Beasts*

1961: Cool Things to Do on a Date besides Neck

NECK . . . and say you didn't.

—Art Unger, *The Cool Book: A Teen-Ager's Guide to Survival in a Square Society*

If you've been trying out all these kissing tips, I assume that you're having a good time. But if you package up all the things you've learned so far about a successful date—having a nice place to go, a well-mannered girl or boy by your side, and a sweet kiss on the front porch at the end of the evening—you might still find one key thing missing. I'll end this chapter with a few thoughts about an important part of any relationship—being able to laugh together. It brings about a good time naturally, and makes you healthier, to boot!

1902: Laughter, a Great Tonic

BEST MEDICINE. We all agree that a good laugh is the best medicine in the world. Physicians have said that no other feeling works so much good to the entire human body as that of merriment. As a digestive, it is unexcelled; as a means of expanding the lungs, there is nothing better. It keeps the heart and face young. It is the best of all tonics to the spirits. It is, too, the most enjoyable of all sensations.

a good laugh makes better friends

BETTER FRIENDS. A good laugh makes better friends with our-selves and everybody around us, and puts us into closer touch with what is best and brightest in our lot in life. It is to be regretted, then, that such a potent agency for our personal good is not more often used.

—Professor B. G. Jefferis, *The Household Guide, or Domestic Cyclopedia*

Chapter Nine
Going Steady

Q Dear Miss Abigail:
Things are going pretty well with this person I've been dating. How do we decide if we should date each other exclusively? I like him, but I'm not sure I'm ready to settle down with just one guy quite yet.

A Quiz time again! If you're thinking about focusing your attentions on just one person, that means you've probably gone out on at least a few dates, so I'd like you to take a moment to see how you are doing. Kay Thomas's *Secrets of Loveliness* contains a delightful quiz to help you determine whether you are a good date. It's written for girls, but boys can have fun with it, too. And just so you don't feel alone, my answers follow the quiz's correct answers, below; I've also included the answers of my book's original owner, Ida Fisher, since she took the time to circle her responses in my copy. Good luck to you, my friends! Once you're done, I'll continue to help you determine whether it's time to settle down with just one guy or gal.

1963: Are You a Good Date?

Test yourself by checking (a), (b), or (c) below:

1.   When alighting from a bus, do you:
      (a) head for the center door right away because that's where
      you're supposed to get off? ____
      (b) wait for your date to step outside so you can go out first?

      ____

      (c) let your date go ahead and help you down? ____

2.   In a restaurant, when a boy asks you what you'd like to eat, do
      you:
      (a) choose the most expensive thing on the menu so he won't
      feel embarrassed? ____
      (b) choose whatever strikes your fancy and then give your
      order to the waiter? ____
      (c) ask the boy what he suggests and then let him give the
      order? ____

3.   At a dance, if a boy is stuck with you, do you:
      (a) decide to stick it out? ____
      (b) suggest you sit out the next one so he can get away grace-
      fully? ____
      (c) try to steer him toward a group of boys and girls, in the
      hope of changing partners? ____

4.   If a boy stands you up on a date, do you:
       (a) announce to all that you're through with him? ____
       (b) blow your top privately next time you meet? ____
       (c) wait for his explanation, and then keep quiet about the whole thing? ____

5.   If your small brother parks in the living room when you have a date, do you:
       (a) attempt to dislodge him by looking daggers at him? ____
       (b) throw him out boldly? ____
       (c) suggest something interesting for him to do? ____

6.   At a movie, if you see two vacant seats do you:
       (a) rush toward them, letting your date follow? ____
       (b) point out the seats and start down the aisle? ____
       (c) wait for him to notice the seats and lead you to them? ____

listen to what your date has to say

7.   At a soda fountain with your date, do you:
       (a) look around to see who else is there so he won't be bored? ____
       (b) keep checking your appearance in the mirror? ____
       (c) listen to what your date has to say? ____

8.   If your mother doesn't like the looks of a boy you date, do you:
     (a) meet him at the corner drugstore? ____
     (b) stop seeing him without an explanation? ____
     (c) ask your mother if you may invite him over so she can get to know him? ____

9.   If your date is picking you up in his car, do you:
     (a) wait until he honks and then rush out? ____
     (b) wait until he rings your doorbell, then go out? ____
     (c) ask him in to meet your parents? ____

10.   When you go out with a new boy, do you:
     (a) tell him about the other boys you date? ____
     (b) fill him in on the latest school gossip? ____
     (c) get him to talk about himself? ____

The answers: (c) in every case. How did you do?
                              —Kay Thomas, *Secrets of Loveliness*

Now for our answers. Ida did quite well, but she missed a few. Seems she has some brushing up to do:

1: (c), 2: (b), 3: (b), 4: (c), 5: (c), 6: (c), 7: (c), 8: (c), 9: (c), 10: (c)

Yours truly failed miserably (oh, well):

1: (a), 2: (b), 3: (huh?), 4: (a), 5: (b), 6: (a), 7: (a), 8: (a), 9: (b), 10: (a)

I know I've been tossing the words "going steady" around, but when exactly was the last time you heard about anyone actually doing so? Much to my dismay, that lingo is long gone. I still like to use it (but then again I like to say "wooing" a lot, too. Wooing! Wooing! Wooing! Oh, sorry, there I go again). Here's a little something to remind you what goin' steady is all about.

1956: Goin' Steady

Rita and Leroy are goin' steady!

How often we hear this said! Dating is an integral part of our American way of living. In most of the world, social relationships between fellows and girls before marriage are frowned upon. The older men and women were young once, found they couldn't trust themselves, and consequently don't trust the young people! Marriages are arranged by the parents, and many a bride doesn't even see the groom until the wedding date. But dating, going steady, engagements with all attendant privileges, are a part of our American freedom.

part of our American freedom

Not that every date means that a fellow and girl are going steady. A fellow should be able to take you to a Youth for Christ rally without thinking he is serious. Enjoy casual dates. When he is ready to go steady, you'll know by his attitude.

—Dorothy Haskin, *Just for Girls*

You may feel pressure from your parents or your peers to settle in and date one guy exclusively, but it's perfectly reasonable to want to see more than one person. Even if things are going particularly well with one boy, you may enjoy yourself just as much with another boy. Rather than rushing to pick one over the other, take some time to get to know each of them better. As long as you're up-front about your intentions and desire to keep your options open, and as long as you're not going the reality-show "date twenty men at a time and publicly crush them as they get booted out of the house" route, it should all work out. Soon enough, you'll find one that you'll want to have a steady relationship with.

1938: The Question of Exclusiveness in Dating

It is usually preferable for young people to have more than one friendship with the opposite sex. It gives them wider basis for comparison and keeps them from tying themselves down prematurely. . . .

When a young man begins to date with a certain girl it sometimes happens that other young men hesitate to cut in and ask the young lady for a date. As a matter of circumstances she is left to exclusive dating with this young man. At times each prefers the company of the other to anyone else, which leads to exclusive dating. Wise young girls will usually be able to ascertain when it is to their advantage or disadvantage to give their time fully to one person. Whether there is exclusive dating or not, every friendship should be kept on a purely friendly basis until the engagement and no friendship should be taken too seriously.

ascertain when it is to their advantage or disadvantage

—Warren D. Bowman, *Home Builders of Tomorrow*

So, you and your sweetheart have decided to go steady after all. It's because you really think she's the one, right? Can't spend a minute without him, eh? Yeah, right. I know the real reason. Easy access to someone to make out with! Here's another on the topic of smooching—this time, the technique is a little more advanced.

1936: The Technique of Kissing

Now is your chance! The moment you feel the tip of your nose touch her scalp, purse your lips and kiss her, the while you inhale a deep breath of air that is redolent with the exquisite odor of her hair. It is then but a few inches to her ear. Touch the rim of her ear with your lips in a sort of brushing motion. Breathe gently into the delicate shell.

Some women react passionately to this subtle act. Brush past her here in this way again and note her reaction. If she draws her head away, return to the hair and sniff luxuriously of it.

Then settle back to her ear, the while you murmur "sweet, airy nothings" into it. From the ear to her neck is but another few inches. Let your lips traverse this distance quickly and then dart into the nape of the neck and, with your lips well pursed, nip the skin there, using the same gentleness as would a cat lifting her precious kittens.

Then, with a series of little nips, bring your lips around from the nape of her neck to the curving swerve of her jaw, close to the ear. Gently kiss the lobe of her ear. But be sure to return to the tender softness of her jaw. From then on, the way should be clear to you. Nuzzle your lips along the soft, downy expanse until you reach the corner of her lips. You will know when this happens because, suddenly, you will feel a strange stiffening of her shoulders under your arm. The reason for this is that the lips constitute one of the main erogenous zones of the body.

All right. You have subtly kissed the corner of her mouth. Don't hesitate. Push on further to more pleasurable spots. Ahead of you lies that which had been promised in your dreams, the tender, luscious lips of the girl you love. But don't sit idly by and watch them quivering.

don't sit idly by and watch them quivering

Act!

Lift your lips away slightly, center them so that when you make contact there will be a perfect union. Notice, only momentarily, the picture of her teeth in her lips, and then, like a seagull swooping gracefully down through the air, bring your lips down firmly onto the lips of the girl who is quivering in your arms.

Kiss her!

Kiss her as though, at that moment, nothing else exists in the world. Kiss her as though your entire life is wrapped up into the period of the kiss. Kiss her as though there is nothing else that you would rather be doing. Kiss her!

—Hugh Morris, *How to Make Love: The Secret of Wooing and Winning the One You Love*

Chapter Ten

Heavy Petting

Q Dear Miss Abigail:

Whoa, things are moving a little fast! I have mixed feelings, and I'm not sure how to handle his advances. What should I do?

A The first selection for you, below, is one that is near and dear to my heart. It kicks off a series of many—hey, this is a passionate topic—classic advice excerpts addressing the hot and frenzied moments of a relationship, and comes from the first book that Miss Abigail ever purchased, Evelyn Millis Duvall's *The Art of Dating* from 1967. Yes, the book that started it all. I hope you'll enjoy this, and come to cherish the phrase "Not now, Ambrose—let's go get a hamburger" as much as I do.

1967: When a Fellow Gets Fresh

When a boy goes beyond what pleases a girl in his lovemaking, she faces a difficult problem. If she allows him to continue, against her wishes, she may be headed for more trouble than she will be able to handle. If she tries to restrain him, she must know how to do it without hurting his feelings or making him feel rejected as a person. This calls for delicate know-how that a girl must learn—in action.

The inexperienced girl may wonder, "If he tries something, shall I slap him and run, or just run?" The more mature girl knows that she doesn't need to resort to either slapping or running in order to deal with the too-amorous boyfriend. She wards off unwelcome behavior with a firm refusal to cooperate, accompanied by a knowing smile and a suggestion of some alternate activity. She may say, "Not now, Ambrose—let's go get a hamburger; I'm hungry."

If he tries something, shall I slap him and run, or just run?

Or she may take a tip from Marianne. When her date seems about to do something objectionable, she takes both his hands in both of hers, squeezes them affectionately, grins into his eyes, and says, "You're quite a guy." By doing this, Marianne lets her date know that she won't go along with his intimacy, at the same time that she shows she likes him as a person.

A girl's best protection is in *anticipating* a situation and deflecting it. The wise girl who wants to avoid a necking session keeps up an animated conversation about things that interest her date until she is returned to her door, when she bids him a pleasant adieu and goes in. This is easier said than accomplished. But if the girl is sure of her objective, she avoids anything that points in another direction. She keeps to brightly lighted, well-populated places and away from dark lonely corners where the situation may get out of hand.

It is a wise girl who knows the variations on the "Come up and see my etchings" theme well enough to decline an invitation to drive to a Lonely Lovers' lane "to see the view." This kind of know-how often comes from talks with other girls. As girls pool their experiences they can share their knowledge of various boys and their approaches. And they learn from each other the skills for dealing with various problem-boy situations.

—Evelyn Millis Duvall, *The Art of Dating*

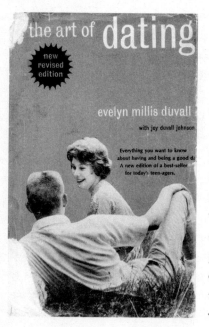

Sometimes it's hard to know if he's serious about you or just kissing you for fun, especially when he's not making any effort to express his feelings verbally. Well, ever heard of "heavy petting"? No, I'm not talking about your dog or cat. You know—making out, snogging, hooking up, friends with benefits—whatever kids these days are calling it. If your date is not displaying affection in any ways other than hot-and-heavy petting sessions, I think you know what his true intentions are.

1956: What Is Petting?

Petting is lovemaking between members of the opposite sex. It produces sexual excitement. The ways of petting are many. Any combination of kissing, caressing, and bodily nearness is commonly called petting. . . .

One might think people pet because they are deeply in love. In reality, there are many other reasons boys and girls make petting a part of their dates. Some think petting is an expected part of dating, and they are afraid of being *that affection which they need and want* different—afraid of not doing the expected thing. Some young people receive very little love from their own family, so petting offers that affection which they need and want, sometimes unconsciously. Boys and girls who have gotten into the habit of petting from some former dating experiences, feel it is the only pattern for dating behavior. Some young people have found the sexual excitement of petting so tempting that they have become absolutely irresponsible and play at petting as a game—a game to be played with any partner available.

—Clyde M. Narramore, *Life and Love: A Christian View of Sex*

1968: How Boys Try to Prove Their Masculinity

To many boys, the proof of masculinity consists in being able to win a girl. In caveman days, men showed their colors by capturing women and dragging them off. In our civilized times, boys try to do much the same by verbal prowess. The boy who can get a girl to fall for his line is often considered a hero. Some boys consider it manly to engage in heavy necking, petting, or even intercourse, not necessarily because they enjoy these things or care about the girl, but because they consider it one way of proving their masculinity to themselves. And that is often why they boast about their accomplish-

they boast about their accomplishments

ments later to other boys. (It also is why some men who are unsure of their own manhood cannot settle down to love one woman. Instead, they flit from one to the other, trying to prove their masculinity to themselves by getting women to succumb to them.) . . .

Let me sum up how most boys want girls to react to them: They want girls to think that they are attractive, smart, and, above all, masculine. They want to be considered strong enough physically, as well as mentally, to protect a girl from danger. They want to be regarded as confident and decisive. And, as I said earlier, they want to be thought of as having those qualities—whatever they may be—which they themselves accept as masculine.

—Tom McGinnis, *A Girl's Guide to Dating and Going Steady*

If you've got serious concerns about what's going on with your relationship, your first instinct may be to try to discuss your feelings with your mom or dad, particularly if you are lucky enough to have parents who are at ease talking about sex with their children. Many parents, however, avoid the topic altogether. They may leave a carefully placed instruction book on a bedside table, or hope that school chums will fill in the gaps of sexual knowledge that they can't bring themselves to explain.

With all the angst about this topic, it's no wonder sex-advice books have proven popular over the years. Casual dialogue in self-help books is a common approach to getting the message across. Mother chats with sis about menstruation; Dad speaks frankly with son about the dangers of drinking. Girls gossip about other girls and boys. A priest discusses the dangers of masturbation with a boy, and countless doctors counsel teenage boys and girls on their "personal problems." If only our family and friends were so at ease! Let's listen in as some high school girls discuss their feelings about going too far.

1961: What about Petting?

"It seems to me that most of the dates I've had, no matter what kind of boys they were with, have been nothing but petting, petting, petting," put in Liz Everett. "I'm getting to where I hate to date, and run the risk of either hurting a boy's feelings by refusing to pet altogether, or letting him go farther than I know he should," and Liz looked generally puzzled. . . .

nothing but petting, petting, petting

"It's either that you've just had bad luck, or else (and I don't mean to be blunt) that you've somehow or other let the idea get around among the boys that you were 'that kind,'" was Janie's comment. "I'll admit that you can't always tell by the way a boy acts before dating you whether he's a wolf in sheep's clothing or a good guy.

"But there's one thing any girl can do," she added. "She can do about boys exactly what boys do about girls. She can talk around and find out how they act on dates, just as they talk around and find out about us. If, after you find that a fellow has a reputation for being a wolf, you go on and date him, in spite of his reputation for going in for heavy petting, you have only yourself to thank, or rather to blame,

when he does what he was advertised as doing, and what you knew
beforehand he was going to do."

—Frank Howard Richardson, *For Young Adults Only: The
Doctor Discusses Your Personal Problems*

1890: Do Not Permit Liberties

Here let me give a word of warning to the maiden herself. Do not
permit any liberties. You know what I mean. Act and expect your
partner to act as though you were in the presence of your parents.
After you are engaged, there is no harm in kissing, but do
not permit any other caresses. You have heard of girls
being seduced, and generally the girl is blamed
most, unjustly though, I think, in most cases.
. . . Be chary even of your kisses. Stand on
your dignity and you are safe.

—"An Old Practitioner" (G. Dallas Lind),
The Mother's Guide and Daughter's Friend

*be chary
even of your
kisses*

Take a look at what the author of the following, James Foster Scott,
writes in the preface of his 1899 book about sex: "This book (intended
primarily and mainly for laymen—not for women or boys) contains
much plain talking, for which I offer no defense."

Scott doesn't say anything about girls, so perhaps it would be all
right (with a man's approval, of course) for a girl to read it aloud to the
forbidden women and boys, so that they too can benefit from the
wisdom of his advice. Just a thought.

Now on to the quote, which, unlike Scott's preface, in this day and age could be considered more on topic than some might prefer.

1899: Influences Which Incite to Sexual Immorality

A thoughtful person cannot help observing that these times are characterized by the reckless abuse of stimulants, material and mental, to which we are fast becoming slavishly addicted. Besides alcoholic stimulants, we are presented at every turn with literary, dramatic, political, artistic, and other excitants which the general public seems to demand for its mental, moral, and physical nourishment. The battle against impurity cannot prevail unless at least the decent members of the community shall have high standards which discountenance sensuality, and unless they demand equal rights for both sexes, and cease to heap up all the degradation on the weaker sex. Virtue in a nation will decline unless its citizens exhibit a zeal for what is pure and good; and no nation can be truly great which does not represent in the aggregate those qualities which are great in the individual.

America, being related to every nation, has derived something good and something evil from all of them; and unless we court a national tragedy, such as those which have blotted out whole empires in the past, we must be awake and active, and demand a due reverence for the family life, while *Something good and* at the same time vigorously opp- *something evil* osing every influence which in any way tends to degrade it. Otherwise we cannot be ascendant and predominant in history. National decay will surely follow if we submit to the seductive influences of the times; and unless we effectively combat the enemies of purity and decency, there is danger that those at least who are city bred will become morally rotten.

—James Foster Scott, *The Sexual Instinct: Its Use and Dangers as Affecting Heredity and Morals*

WARNING: THE FOLLOWING EXCERPT IS FOR MATURE AUDIENCES ONLY. All these warnings about the dangers of petting and kissing are getting me down. It can't be all bad, can it? How about some pro-petting advice for those who really, really want to?

1949: Plunging In

There are times, of course, when sex sneaks up—even on "nice" people—very unexpectedly. Healthy exuberance, which may or may not have been heightened by alcohol, physical chemistry, and a warm spring (or summer) night (or cool autumn night, or cold winter night) may conspire to work together to produce surprising and unforeseen results. The only excuse either or both can think of when they face themselves sheepishly the next day are those classic, all-embracing words: "It seemed the thing to do at the time."

It is hard to determine how many girls allow this exuberance to trip them. And furthermore, heart-to-heart talks with them seldom if ever do any good because they never intend to be tripped anyway. Probably not many approach sex in this manner. It is too Serious a Business to most women who feel that they have to get their thoughts on the matter all sorted out before proceeding. . . .

The adventurous young woman who is wondering whether to plunge in, even though she is not in love (or at least not yet), has many angles to consider. She is fond of the chap and there is certainly sizzling attraction

who is she to pass up anything so earthshaking?

between them, even though she does not feel he would be ideal to have around for the rest of her life. She has no yearnings to keep his shirt buttons anchored or pick up his wet bath towels. But she is intensely curious about sex and all the superlatives which have been expended on it ever since she can remember. If her background has been strict, it was the Ultimate Sin. If her reading has been of wide scope and her imagination sensitive, she has come to feel that it is Life's Great Experience and who is she to pass up anything so earthshaking? Besides, our society is artificial anyway, and our sex mores have arisen out of economic exigencies. The Samoans—or one of those tribes—go for free love and everybody's happy. Who is to say that we are right and they are wrong and isn't it all relative? She has heard about frustrations and how dangerous they are and heaven knows she feels plenty frustrated. Doesn't she owe it to herself to take the cure, when the cure is so simple?

—Jean Van Evera, *How to Be Happy While Single*

1916: Liberties before Marriage

Kissing, embracing, sitting in lover's lap, leaning on his breast, long periods of secluded companionship, are dangerous conditions. Thoughtful parents should have a profound fear at the dangers surrounding such a state of affairs. It is a marvel that so many ladies arrive safely at the wedding day. If our young women realized the danger of arousing the sexuality even of the best men, they would shudder at the risk they run. Don't do it, ladies!

—Professor T. W. Shannon, *Nature's Secrets Revealed: Scientific Knowledge of the Laws of Sex Life and Heredity, or Eugenics*

Chapter Eleven

It's Not You, It's Me

Q   Dear Miss Abigail:

Things aren't really working out as planned. He just sent me an "It's not you, it's me!" e-mail. Are we doomed?

A   That certainly isn't a good sign. I'm so sorry it had to happen over e-mail! I'm sure everyone has at least one story of being unceremoniously dumped, either privately or in public. You know, like that time my, um, "friend" was dumped on the up escalator of a subway station in Washington, D.C., in front of a crowd of tourists and government workers heading home? Not fun.

Alas, there are times when relationships are just not meant to be, and as things end, someone usually gets hurt in the process. To cheer us all up, I've pulled out two complementary excerpts from the wonderful Nina Farewell, who wrote *The Unfair Sex: An Exposé of the Human Male for Young Women of Most Ages* in 1953. The first is from the perspective of a woman who has been dumped. In the second, Farewell flips it and the woman is the dumper.

1953: Why Didn't I Hear from Him Again?

This plaintive cry has echoed in the heart of every woman at some time or other in her life. Even the most glamorous, the most sought after, are faced with the enigma of the man who seems captivated, and yet never calls again.

There are two important types from whom one does not hear again. Type I takes you and then drops you. Type II takes your phone number and never uses it.

Why? Why do such awful things happen? And what can be done to prevent them? Let us first examine the causes, which are the same in either case.

Ask yourself if you committed any of the following errors:

Did you talk too much?

Did you talk about marriage?

Did you make him spend too much?

Did you make him feel inferior?

Did you boast?

Did you laugh too loud or chew too hard?

Did you accept him too eagerly?

Did you refuse him too definitely?

Did you laugh too loud or chew too hard?

On the other hand, your failure may have nothing to do with you at all—not with your appearance, your personality, your behavior, nor with the fact that you did or did not give yourself.

Often you have done nothing wrong, but are merely the victim of circumstances beyond your control. . . .

—Nina Farewell, *The Unfair Sex: An Exposé of the Human Male for Young Women of Most Ages*

1953: How to Drop a Man without Hurting Him

This operation is considered by some women to be as pleasing
as that of Refusing. How lovely it is to reach the end and
realize you got there first! Whether you have retained
your chastity or made the tactical blunder of
giving it all—in either case, the pleasure is now
yours. You are about to circumvent the awful
jolt of being dropped by a man. . . . If you wish
to get rid of him because he has begun to bore you,

*it only
prolongs the
agony*

or you have found someone else, or you suspect he will never propose—
deal with him kindly. After all, he is human, he has shared many
pleasant hours with you—and besides, you may want him back
someday. . . .

Your behavior should be lovable in the extreme. Allow no callous
note to creep into your voice. Make him think he is losing a desirable,
adorable girl—not a fickle one. Do not reproach him with any past

offense. Say it has all been lovely. Tell him you will remember him as one of the nicest people you ever knew. In other words, send him on his way with a sympathetic smile and a warm handshake.

What reason do you give? Certainly not the truth. If he has begun to bore you, be kind enough to conceal this fact from him. Few things can be more wounding to a man's ego. Tell him instead that your mother thinks you are seeing too much of him. . . .

do not permit yourself to be unhappy for him

In any event, when you undertake to sever relations with a man, do not permit yourself to be unhappy for him. Such sentimentality is misplaced. The fact that he belongs to the male sex is proof positive that he has deeply wounded, or will one day wound, some or many women. The pain you are inflicting is well earned.

And remember—in any romance which does not result in marriage, one of the two people involved must inevitably get dropped. Be thankful that this time it is not you.

—Nina Farewell, *The Unfair Sex: An Exposé of the Human Male for Young Women of Most Ages*

1969: Make It Final

A broken heart is like a broken vase; it mends more easily when the break is clean. A gradual separation is always tempting—it seems so much easier at first—but it only prolongs the agony. Vacillation saps your strength and makes the recovery period longer . . . and far more depressing. When you reach the point where only a few weak threads tie you together, it's best to sever them completely.

Until you do, you won't be able to cast a new line in another direction.

—Rebecca E. Greer, *Why Isn't a Nice Girl Like You Married?*
Or, How to Get the Most out of Life While You're Single

1880: Duty of a Rejected Suitor

*accept
the lady's
decision
as final*

The duty of the rejected suitor is quite clear. Etiquette demands that he shall accept the lady's decision as final and retire from the field. He has no right to demand the reason of her refusal. If she assign it, he is bound to respect her secret, if it is one, and to hold it inviolable.

To persist in urging his suit or to follow up the lady with marked attentions would be in the worst possible taste. The proper course is to withdraw as much as possible from the circles in which she moves, so that she may be spared reminiscences which cannot be other than painful.

—John A. Ruth, *Decorum: A Practical Treatise on Etiquette
and Dress of the Best American Society*

Feeling bad about the breakup? Have you tried ice cream? Chocolate bars? Sobbing on the shoulder of your best friend? There, there. That's better.

1911: A Broken Heart

HEALING. The paralyzing and agonizing consequences of ruptured love can only be remedied by
diversion and society. Bring the mind into a state

the pangs of disappointment in love

of patriotic independence with a full determination to
blot out the past. Those who cannot bring into subordination the pangs of disappointment in love are not strong characters, and invariably will suffer disappointments in almost every department of life. . . .

RISE ABOVE IT. Cheer up! If you cannot think pleasurably over your misfortune, forget it. You must do this or perish. Your power and influence is too much to blight by foolish and melancholic pining. Your own sense, your self-respect, your self-love, your love for others, command you not to spoil yourself by crying over "spilt milk."

LOVE AGAIN. As love was the cause of your suffering, so love again will restore you, and you will love better and more consistently. Do not allow yourself to become soured and detest and shun association. Rebuild your dilapidated sexuality by cultivating a general appreciation of the excellence, especially of the mental and moral qualities of the opposite sex. Conquer your prejudices, and vow not to allow anyone to annoy or disturb your calmness.

—Professor B. G. Jefferis and J. L. Nichols, *Search Lights on Health: Light on Dark Corners: A Complete Sexual Science and a Guide to Purity and Physical Manhood, Advice to Maiden, Wife and Mother, Love, Courtship and Marriage*

Chapter Twelve
On Being Single

Q Dear Miss Abigail:
My parents and friends are worried about me, but really, I'm fine being single, really . . . (sob) . . . I am . . . (sob) . . .

A Oh, sweetie, I believe you—and so do my authors. A number of books in my collection are written with the single woman (and every now and then the single man) in mind. This section is devoted to those out there who are between relationships, whether miserably or happily, by choice or pure circumstance. The first excerpt is from a great book titled *How to Be Happy While Single.* I just know it'll cheer you up.

1949: A Girl's Best Friend

Nothing cheers up a girl faster, when she has the whoops and the jangles, than contemplating the Ex-Men of Her Life. Think over your departed admirers. Would you really want to be fighting over the hills with the tightwad who walked you eleven blocks *the whoops and the jangles* in the rain one night rather than take a taxi? How pleasant would life be with the Gloomy Gus whose disposition resembled that of a discontented chow dog? The D.T.'s finally caught up with the otherwise top-notch chap you were seriously considering marrying several years ago, hesitating only because you doubted his ability to control his drinking. Others flit across your mind: the irresponsible spirit who put on the women's hats at a party and pulled chairs out from under people; the hypochondriac who carried his thermometer with him and took his temperature, publicly or privately, every hour; and others who were just plain dull, never thinking an interesting thought or expressing an original idea. If you'd married one of them at least you wouldn't be "lonely" as you now think you are—and what a heavenly state loneliness would seem. Most of these men eventually married other women, so you realize that no man is so hopeless that some woman won't marry him. Now you are paying the price for being discriminating, but actually you are solitary, not lonely. Always remember that solitude is voluntary, loneliness is involuntary.

Probably these ruminations over the past have put you in a state of mind to do something constructive about the present. How do you go about filling the vacuum? There are many ways, and the wonderful part of the "cure" is that it will enrich every phase of your life, whether lonely, solitary, or full. If you ever become an "island" again, as you probably will, married or single, you won't have to start from scratch learning how to be your own best friend.

—Jean Van Evera, *How to Be Happy While Single*

1938: Find a Desirable Outlet

The severest stress on the single person comes from the blocking of emotional outlets. Thus it behooves those who remain single to take special care that their personalities are not warped by single life. This is just as true of the men as the women, for bachelors often develop peculiar habits and traits. Single people need a desirable emotional outlet which can often be found in social service. Thousands of single women today are doubtless sublimating their maternal tendency in such vocations as teaching, nursing, and social work. These fields are often blessed by having women in them who have a strong maternal tendency, since they are likely to be more sympathetic toward the unfortunate. Some of the greatest contributions to human welfare have come from men and women who have converted their disappointments and suffering into a force for social betterment.

In making one's adjustment to single life it is always wise to avoid self-pity. It is far better to find others who are more

unfortunate than oneself and make life pleasant
for them. It is also healthy to take a vital
interest in the life around one.

*it is always
wise to avoid
self-pity*

It is perhaps wise for young women
especially to think of what they may do
in case they do not marry. They may plan
two careers: marriage, in case the right person comes along, and
another career which they may follow in case they do not marry.
The mentally healthy person who has planned for years in this
dual manner will not likely be so disappointed if she never marries, but will be able to make a happy adjustment in some worthy
vocation.

—Warren D. Bowman, *Home Builders of Tomorrow*

Dorothy Dix's words on the dateless girl offer some important food for
thought. Ms. Dix certainly doesn't sound too keen on marriage, does
she? Tee hee.

1939: The Girl Who Has No Dates

The plight of the girls who have a natural feminine yearning for the
attentions of men and love and romance and marriage but who are denied
these is truly a sad one. What makes this situation still more pathetic
is that they exaggerate their value and the happiness they would bring
them. The girl who has no dates pictures every party as a wild orgy of
joy. She imagines every man is a Prince Charming and she has never a
doubt but that if she did marry her husband would be an ideal mate and
her home an earthly paradise.

It never seems to occur to these girls that most of the parties are dull, stupid affairs where the guests yawn in each other's faces; that the boyfriend, too, is often a bore who reduces a girl to tears and with whom she goes out only in the hope of meeting some more entertaining companion. Nor does she suspect that on their wedding days most wives do not enter into an Elysium but get life sentences at hard work.

If the business girl will look around at her married friends she will see that most of them look older than she does; that few of them are as well-dressed

DREAMING OF THE FUTURE.

or can afford the amusements she enjoys. And she will discover that the husband who remains a gallant lover after three or four years of married life is about as rare as hens' teeth.

For most women marriage is doing without pretty clothes and is hard work and childbearing and walking colicky babies and putting up with the temper and crotchets of a man who generally is disillusioned with matrimony himself. So the average engaged girl who thinks she is going to miss all the trials and tribulations of matrimony and draw the capital prize is simply fooling herself.

Still, all of this does not keep girls from wanting to marry or their mothers from wanting to see them married. That is nature, with which we cannot argue, and the pity of it is that there is not some way by which a miracle could be wrought to provide proper bridegrooms for all these nice girls who would make such good wives. . . .

It seems to me there are only two things these matrimony-minded girls can do, especially after they have reached the age of thirty, when time becomes a great factor in success. One is boldly to take the initiative and do the courting themselves; pick out the particular men they desire to have for husbands and go in for a whirlwind campaign. Virtually any woman can marry any man if she will just go after him hard enough, provided she never lets him suspect that she is being the aggressor. . . .

[What] can the girl do whom boys never date up of their own voli-tion, whose partners have to be conscripted for her at dances and who knows herself to be an undesired addition to any party she wishes her-self upon?

Before succumbing to the inevitable, she might give herself one more chance by making a change in her environment. Many a girl who is a social failure at home is a success abroad. Many a girl whom the boys on Main Street couldn't see becomes one whom strange men behold with admira-tion, as is witnessed by the number of girls who marry away from home. If, however, a girl finds that threshing in different water brings no fish rising to her bait, then she saves herself mortification and wear and tear on her soul and body if she accepts the situation, gives up the struggle to attract men, and fills her life with other interests.

no fish rising to her bait

—Dorothy Dix, *How to Win and Hold a Husband*

1969: To Live without Sex

If I must live without sex, Lord, help me do so gracefully. Don't let me become bitter and resentful, blaming you, the world, or anyone else.

Instead of self-pity, give me the strength and the cheerful acceptance that comes from self-respect.

don't let me become bitter

Above all, give me the understanding, the wisdom to sort out complexities of this common human condition. It's so easy to confuse what the body thinks it needs and wants with what the mind and the world dictate. Protect me from this confusion, Lord, don't let me be misled.

Help me to remember, Lord, that many people endure afflictions and deprivations far worse. And that a great many people live happy, purposeful, inspiring lives that are devoid of sex.

Give me their secrets of acceptance, give me their grace.

If I am to live without sex, Lord, allow me to express and use this great force you have given me for some significant end.

—Marjorie Holmes, *I've Got to Talk to Somebody, God*

I know what you're thinking. Here is Miss Abigail, trying to cheer you up and make it sound like singledom is the best thing that could ever happen to a person (or at least a thing that can be tolerated). But all the while, you're imagining life as an old maid, possibly living with thirteen or fourteen cats, a few scruffy dogs, and a guinea pig, up in the old house on the hill. I know, pretty darn sad.

Well, snap out of it and read this, from twentieth-century exercise guru Bernarr Macfadden. He offers up some pro-singles-adoption advice from 1923—apparently, it's having some kids around the house that stops people from labeling you an old maid. Not reducing the number of your cats.

1923: The Old Maid

Some few years ago the phrase "bachelor girl" was a popular one, and we still have her with us, though the name is less used. The bachelor girl is an unmarried woman, of almost any age, who has gone out into the world of business and is leading her own independent, and generally very efficient, life. She carries with her no suggestion of failure. No one could ever think of her as a remnant on life's bargain counter. She has remained unmarried because no man came into her circle of friends who possessed enough attractions to woo her from a life of "single blessedness." It would sometimes seem to be something of a reflection upon the men of the present time, when one looks over the women who would have made such splendid mothers, but who have persistently remained outside of the bonds of matrimony. The bachelor girl has managed to escape the narrow life and wizened existence of the traditional old maid, but has she after all nothing to regret?

her ambitions have full sway

There are many allurements in the single life. There is, for example, the greater freedom which comes to one who has no one's needs or desires to consider but her own. She can live her own life, which is what so many of us clamor for in the early years of adolescence. She is free to let her ambitions have full sway, and she may, therefore, achieve

success—in some instances a noteworthy one. Yet we may ask ourselves, Is she always satisfied?

While she is young and everything comes her way, she is too busy
climbing from one point to the next on life's ladder to ask herself this
question. When she reaches middle life and finds that she has achieved
all that she dreamed of, and possibly more, there is little room for this
question. But as the shadows of life begin to gather around her, and
she finds herself left more and more alone because those of her own
generation are silently departing to other shores, more and more frequently must the question return to her, "Is this all? Has it been
worthwhile?". . .

Although they may never know the intimate joys of marriage, there
is no reason why they should be deprived of the deep and lasting happiness of motherhood. Without any doubt, the greatest, the most
lasting, most satisfying happiness that comes to woman, comes through
the gratification of her maternal instinct, and it need not necessarily be
her own children who bring to her this satisfaction. There are today
thousands of little children left orphans because of war, and no woman
need ever be without little children in her home. . . . There will be no
drying up of the fountain of life as the years go by, but rather will it
grow richer and fuller from year to year. Thus may the bachelor girl
insure herself against the dreaded fate of ever becoming that pitiful
creature, the traditional old maid.

—Bernarr Macfadden, *Womanhood and Marriage.*

Once you do get through the pain of a breakup, I think you'll
agree that there is no pleasure greater than that of sleeping alone.
As a supreme lover of sleep and bedtime and hitting the snooze

button as many times as I like without someone else complaining about it, I would have to agree with the following:

1936: Pleasures of a Single Bed

Think of the things that you, all alone, don't have to do. You don't have to turn out your light when you want to read, because somebody else wants to sleep. You don't have to have the light on when you want to sleep, because somebody else wants to read. You don't have to get up in the night to fix somebody else's hot-water bottle, or lie awake listening to snores, or be vivacious when you're tired, or cheerful when you're blue, or sympathetic when you're bored. You probably have your bathroom all to yourself, too, which is unquestionably one of Life's Great Blessings. You don't have to wait till someone finishes shaving, when you are all set for a cold-cream session. You have no one complaining about your pet bottles, no one to drop wet towels on the floor, no one occupying the bathtub when you have just time to take a shower. From dusk until dawn, you can do exactly as you please, which, after all, is a pretty good allotment in this world where a lot of conforming is expected of everyone.

you can do exactly as you please

—Marjorie Hillis, *Live Alone and Like It: A Guide
for the Extra Woman*

All talk of bachelor girls and single beds aside, I'm optimistic that true love will find you once more. Self-esteem and confidence are the keys

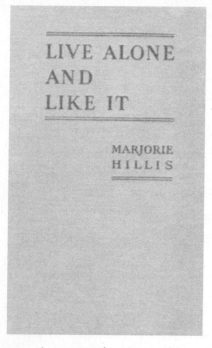

LIVE ALONE
AND
LIKE IT

MARJORIE
HILLS

to getting through this time of transition from one relationship to another. You've got to look on the bright side, and keep your eyes open for the next streetcar to come barreling down the tracks toward your life.

1933: Men Are Like Streetcars

The girl who has many friends, who is liked by her own sex as well as by the opposite sex, who is as attractive as nature and her own efforts can make her and does not strive overmuch to impress men with her beauty or brains or popularity, can almost leave results to Cupid. She may be agreeably encouraging to a young man whom she likes. There is a vast distinction between running after a man and repulsing him at every opportunity or expecting him to prove his devotion by some unreasonable attention or gift. The beautiful lady who expected her lover to demonstrate his love by fetching her glove out of the lion's den got the glove—and a scathing speech of farewell by the lover.

If a man loves a girl he will tell her so without the performance of any tricks or subtle schemes on her part. If he does not, well, as Maudie remarks (in *Men Are Like Street Cars*, by Graeme and Sarah

Lorimer), "Men are like streetcars, there is always another one coming."

    —Catherine Atkinson Miller, *Eighteen: The Art of Being a Woman*

1929: Make Success Visible

Saturate your mind with hope, the expectation of better things, with the belief that your dreams are coming true. Be convinced that you are going to win out; let your mind rest with success thoughts. Don't let the enemies of your success and happiness dominate in your mind or they will bring to you the condition they represent.

saturate your mind with hope

    —Edith Mae Cummings, *Pots, Pans and Millions*

Chapter Thirteen

It'll Happen When You Least Expect It

Q   Dear Miss Abigail:

I can't stand it when people say, "Don't worry—you'll meet someone when you least expect it!" Am I just being a crank?

A   Does this drive you crazy, too? "Just think positively!" or how about, "No one will love you unless you love yourself!" I bet that one gets on your nerves, too. Well, sorry, you're going to have to think some happy thoughts. And I've got just the thing to help.

1923: **Creative Thoughts, Happy Thoughts**

If you have memories of sadness and remorse of the past, banish them from the mind. Refuse to think of them, and they are gone forever. Drive from your mind all memories that are connected with failures of the past. Drive out all doubts and fears and gloom forebodings

Do not put off until tomorrow the banishment of your dead hopes, but brush them overboard now.

Shun anything that even has the earmarks of evil. Let nothing corrupt your thoughts. Bear not the scepter of defeat. "He is the assassin of Victory."

the banishment of your dead hopes

There is a simple way to do this. Every day is followed by tomorrow and tomorrow can be as you wish it to be. You can feed the mind tomorrow on the same ideas it has in the past or entirely different ones.

Resolve tonight, that when you awake in the morning you are going to think creative thoughts, happy thoughts. Say to your inner self, "Be on watch. Let no thoughts enter that are not of an upbuilding nature."

—Arthur Gould and E. E. and M. A. Dodson. *How to Obtain Your Desires: Positive Thoughts Attract Success*

1922: **A Sunny Disposition**

Every girl must meet her share of bumps in life. If they do not come soon they must come late. It is impossible that she should pass through life in the sunshine all the time. She must have her share of shadow. She cannot escape it. But it is not the deep shadows that generally cloud a girl's life, and make her unhappy and sullen. It is the little

pass these little bumps and keep sweet

things, insignificant in themselves, and which could have been passed by with hardly a thought if resisted one by one, that irritate the temper and mar the happiness. Every day our girl will meet with circumstances in which she has her choice between frowning and sending back a stinging retort, or smiling and passing them by with a kind word. If she can pass these little bumps and keep sweet, then she has mastered the art of being sunny.

—Mabel Hale, *Beautiful Girlhood*

Now that you've got your attitude adjusted, you might start thinking about getting back into the swing of things. We'll ease into this, don't worry. I want to see you out there, meeting a new dream date—but at your own pace. When you're ready, here's some advice for getting back into the dating scene.

1949: Meeting Men

Suppose your friends, married, single, old or young, male or female, know absolutely not one stray extra man. Then what? Your work, your office? None there, either. What next?

There are hobby clubs, church groups, evening classes, and sports. But here is the catch. You have to choose something in which your interest is genuine. Women who suddenly start going to church for the

choose something in which your interest is genuine

purpose of "meeting men" usually have it written on their faces that the Lord is not their primary concern. The girl who loathes the outdoors but joins a hiking club because she has heard there are "men" in it is not a very stimulating companion, and besides she gives herself away. Where evening classes are concerned, the subjects in which most women are usually interested—drama, languages, and the arts—do not attract many men. When a man decides to go to night school after a hard day's work he usually does it for one reason: to better himself in his job and increase his earning power. He enrolls for international law, economics, or calculus review. If a woman is sincere in her passion to pick up her calculus again she probably will find lots of men. But she makes a fool of herself if she goes into something for which she obviously has no interest, talent, or proficiency.

But all is by no means lost. If you make yourself a more interesting person by means of further study, someone eventually is sure to appreciate you.

—Jean Van Evera, *How to Be Happy While Single*

1901: On the Selection of Life Partners

A woman should avoid accepting a man who has been particularly successful with women. At the same time, she should look for one to whom woman is not an enigma, and who is a man of the world and of strong character, so that she may feel sure that when he chose her, he said to himself: "I know my mind; happiness for me lies there." On that man she will be able to depend and lean safely. . . .

shun a dragon of virtue

I should advise women to shun a dragon of virtue like fire: she should prefer a dragoon rather. A man may be good, but he must not overdo it. He that has no wickedness is too good for this world; not even a nun could endure him. Fancy, my dear lady, a man being shocked by you! The male prig is the abomination of the earth, and should be the pet aversion of women.

—Max O'Rell, *Her Royal Highness Woman and His Majesty—Cupid*

1946: Live Dangerously!

Above all, learn to live dangerously! Life is very short, and the precious minutes seep through the hourglass with unseemly haste. All the more reason why you should put aside the bogeys and taboos that you accepted uncritically in your youth, and seek that which you need to fulfill your life. Seek it bravely.

put aside the bogeys and taboos

Do not defer living any longer. Take chances! It is better to take chances, it is better to try, to fail, and to try again—if you are certain of your goal—than to remain in cowardly and unhappy security to live out aeons of regret for lost opportunities.

—W. Béran Wolfe, *A Woman's Best Years: The Art of Staying Young*

Take a deep breath. Ready to move on now? Go back to chapter 6 of this book for guidance through a repeat of the dating cycle. (I'm assuming you can skip chapters 4 and 5, because you're a pro by now!) I'll see you back here after you've found someone that seems to be sticking around for good. Trust me, you'll be back.

Chapter Fourteen
Falling in Love

Q   Dear Miss Abigail:
I might be crazy, but I think I'm actually falling in love!
How can I tell if it's for real?

A   Unfortunately, there is no one mark by which you can
identify true love—it's up to you to discover the magical
potion. Is it love? Is it lust? Or is it just a silly old crush?
Let's ponder these questions with more advice from our
friend Dorothy Dix.

1939: How to Tell Whether You Are in Love

If you never weary of a man's company, even when he talks about himself by the hour; if you can play games together without quarreling; if you can spend a rainy weekend in the country without talking yourselves out and getting on each other's nerves; then you may be sure that you have the love that is foolproof and will stand the wear and tear of matrimony.

Then, if you are still in doubt whether or not you are in love with a man, concentrate on his faults and magnify them and see whether they outweigh his virtues as far as you are concerned. Consider whether or not his little personal peculiarities irritate you. Could you stand listening to his pet stories over and over again for the remainder of your life? Do you feel that you could take a never-ending heart-interest in the grocery trade? How about having to live with a man who carries his small change in a purse with a lock on it and who is a little closefisted? You like books and symphony concerts, while he never reads anything but the headlines in the newspapers and the comic strip and has a jazz taste in music. What about it?

concentrate on his faults and magnify them

If he bores you at times until you feel like screaming, and if you think that the first thing you will do after you marry him is going to be on the reformation side, you don't really love him. There is no truer test of love than to love the faults of a dear one, and to think of them tenderly as being just amusing traits of individuality because they are his.

—Dorothy Dix, *How to Win and Hold a Husband*

You may be feeling pretty strong emotions for the person you are dating. But how can you tell the difference between real love and puppy love?

1965: Puppy Love

Diane and Don were both shy teenagers when they found themselves seated next to one another at a church social. Soon they discovered they enjoyed talking together and that they felt less self-conscious in crowds when they were with each other.

they miss one another terribly when apart

They began going steady and they liked to do things together. . . . Each feels more self-confident when with the other, and they miss one another terribly when apart. They feel they are "in love," yet realize they are much too young to be sure this is the love on which a successful marriage could be based. Until they are sure one way or the other, they'll continue their good times and companionship.

This is the love of the early teens. For weeks Jeff and Julie are sure they are in love. Songs like "Too Young" have great appeal for them. They are together constantly: on the phone, in person, passing notes in school, through daydreams (and night dreams, too). Then gradually, or perhaps suddenly, they find their interest in one another is dwindling and a new interest replaces it.

Again, this is normal and nothing to be laughed at. As evangelist Billy Graham has pointed out, "Don't scoff at puppy love. It's very real to the puppies!"

—Letha Scanzoni, *Youth Looks at Love*

1898: Love's Beginnings

they are won by some slight thing

Very slight things are sufficient for love's beginnings. A girl puts on a pretty gown, knots a blue ribbon at her throat, sticks a flower in her belt, and goes lightly and thoughtlessly along her way, and that day a man happens to see the bright cheek and the blue ribbon, and loses his heart. We have all heard of the maiden who tied her bonnet under her chin and tied a young man's heart within, and most of us, when we remember cases of love at first sight, see that what was so apparently accidental had a good deal to do with the matter. As a rule, young people do not say to themselves, "Go to, I will seek a mate." On the contrary, they are won by some slight thing; some grace of manner, or charm of speech, a dimple, a blush, a soft word, and before they know it, all is over with them, so far as love is concerned.

—Margaret E. Sangster, *The Art of Home Making*

Is it a case of love at first sight? Maybe, and we're not saying that there's anything wrong with that. Well, I'm not. Mr. Ruth may have other ideas.

1880: Love at First Sight

No doubt there is such a thing as love at first sight, but love alone is a very uncertain foundation upon which to base marriage. There should be thorough acquaintanceship and a certain knowledge of harmony of tastes and temperaments before matrimony is ventured upon.

—John A. Ruth, *Decorum: A Practical Treatise on Etiquette and Dress of the Best American Society*

1916: Love a Beautifier!

Love has the power to transfigure face and form. Homely, indeed, must be the face which is not made pleasing by love's enchanting influence. It gives roundness to the form, grace to the movements, light to the eye, sweetness to the mouth, color to the cheek, and animation to the whole figure. Every organ of the body

the power to transfigure face and form

seems imbued by it with new life, and every function is rendered more efficient. To the face of many a pale-cheeked girl have three sweet words brought the rosy hue of health and beauty.

—Professor T. W. Shannon, *Nature's Secrets Revealed: Scientific Knowledge of the Laws of Sex Life and Heredity, or Eugenics.*

Girl loves boy. Boy loves girl. Before you take that next step, though, you might want to ask some important questions about each other. Why not model your situation after the wonderful caveman era? I'm sure this is *exactly* like your own relationship.

1928: The Growth of Love

The young woman studies a certain young man who is paying her a great deal of attention, and intuitively she asks herself the same questions that the cavewoman

Will he provide the family with skins and fire and cattle to milk?

asked. Is this man strong and brave? If other men come to the cave, will he be willing to fight them and be able to win? Can he hunt so there will always be a lot of meat to eat? Will he provide the family with skins and fire and cattle to milk? Will he be kind to the baby? Is he the kind of man that will stay in the cave at night? Is he a one-woman or a many-woman man? Is he healthy or sick? What kind of a tribe did he come from? Was his father good to the women and children? Has he ever been able to save any skins and accumulate any cattle and grain and dried fish? Is he a spender or a saver? Last of all, does he really desire me so much that he wants me for all of his life? Or will he be tired of me when I have the first baby?

While she is by his side in the automobile he is asking himself a similar set of questions about her. The fact that they are going sixty miles an hour does not keep him from thinking, Is this woman strong and true? If I am away from the cave and other men come, will she fight them or love them? If I bring meat and food home, will she be able to cook them so they taste good and their eating makes me strong to hunt some more? Or shall I have a constant pain inside? Will she be able to cook like Mother does? (Better stop asking that, young man, or trouble will begin!) Will she be willing and able to keep the fire burning and make the butter and see that the skins are dry and clean? When I come back from the hunt, will she be in the cave or running around, talking to that red-headed woman? Will she want to have babies and can she take care of a baby so that it will not die? Is she a one-man woman? Would she rather be home than anywhere else? What kind of woman was her mother—how about her tribe? If I accumulate property, will she be able to care for it? Finally, do I want her for a wife? Or shall I be sick of her and she of me a few months after we are married?

When young people begin to ask themselves such questions, they are in love.

—David H. Keller, *Love, Courtship, Marriage*

1916: Two Souls Come Together

When two souls come together, each seeking to magnify the other, each in subordinate sense worshiping the other, each help the other; the two flying together so that each wing-beat of the one helps each wing-beat of the other—

each wing-beat of the one helps each wing-beat of the other when two souls come together thus, they are lovers. They who unitedly move themselves away from grossness and from earth, toward the throne crystalline and the pavement golden, are, indeed, true lovers.

—Professor B. G. Jefferis and J. L. Nichols, *Search Lights on Health: Light on Dark Corners: A Complete Sexual Science and a Guide to Purity and Physical Manhood, Advice to Maiden, Wife and Mother, Love, Courtship and Marriage*

How perfectly dramatic is this next excerpt! Which is appropriate, given that the author, Elinor Glyn, not only wrote advice books and romances, but was also launching a career as a Hollywood producer, writer, and director of films at about the time she penned this in the 1920s.

1923: Ideal Love

Being *in love* is merely a physical state of exaltation; *loving* is the merging of the spirit which at its white heat has glorified the physical instinct for re-creating into a godlike beatitude not of earth. Loving throbs with delight in the flesh; it thrills the spirit with reverence; it glorifies into beauty commonplace things; it draws nearer in sickness and sorrow, and is not the sport of change. When a woman loves truly she has the passion of the mistress, the selfless tenderness of the mother, the dignity and devotion of the wife. She is all fire and snow, all wile and frankness, all passion and reserve; she is authoritative and obedient— Queen and Child.

And a man ceases to be a brute, and becomes a God!

Love is beautiful and terrible—and vital. It gilds dark places, and turns stones into jewels. It is tender enough to be of the Angels, and warm enough to be of the Sun. Love is *tangible*. It means to be close—close—to be clasped—to be touching—to be One!

love is beautiful and terrible—and vital

Of all the emotions which Human beings feel, Love is the most divine.

It is the vital spark which makes life, it is the expression of the soul. The lowest creatures, the worst characters, are raised when they love— because for the time it holds them under its sway they cease to be utterly selfish. Love is Nature's glorious manifestation of the unconscious desire to re-create love's likeness. It invests the mere animal instinct for species-preservation with all the beauties of the imagination. It is an essence beyond our sight, or hearing, or touch, which uplifts us.

—Elinor Glyn, *The Philosophy of Love*

Guys: now that you are sure you love her dearly, you may be trying to figure out what to say in that love letter. Here are some sample letters to get you started. Although I said before that e-mail is an appropriate means of correspondence while dating, you'll likely score more points if you write on actual paper and deliver your letter by hand or through the post. Trust me, she'll think more highly of you when she receives something that can be savored, held, sniffed, and slipped under her pillow.

1911: Letter Writing

Any extravagant flattery should be avoided, both as tending to disgust those to whom It is addressed, as well as to degrade the writers, and to create suspicion as to their sincerity. The sentiments should spring from the tenderness of the heart, and, when faithfully and delicately expressed, will never be read without exciting sympathy or emotion in all hearts not absolutely deadened by insensitivity.

Declaration of Affection

Dear Nellie:

Will you allow me, in a few plain and simple words, respectfully to express the sincere esteem and affection I entertain for you, and to ask whether I may venture to hope that these sentiments are returned? I love you truly and earnestly, and knowing you admire frankness and candor in all things, I cannot think that you will take offense at this letter. Perhaps it is self-flattery to suppose I have any place in your regard. Should this be so, the error will carry with it its own punishment, for my happy dream will be over. I will try to think otherwise, however, and shall await your answer with hope. Trusting soon to hear from you, I remain, dear Nellie,

Sincerely Yours,
J. L. Master

An Ardent Declaration

My Dearest Laura:

I can no longer restrain myself from writing to you, dearest and best of girls, what I have often been on the point of saying to you. I love you so much that I cannot find words in which to express my feelings. I have loved you from the very first day we met, and always shall. Do you blame me because I write so freely? I should be unworthy of you if I did not

Oh, Laura, can you love me in return?

tell you the whole truth. Oh, Laura, can you love me in return? I am sure I shall not be able to bear it if your answer is unfavorable. I will study your every wish if you will give me the right to do so. May I hope? Send just one kind word to your sincere friend,

Harry Smith

—Professor B. G. Jefferis and J. L. Nichols, *Search Lights on Health: Light on Dark Corners: A Complete Sexual Science and a Guide to Purity and Physical Manhood, Advice to Maiden, Wife and Mother, Love, Courtship and Marriage*

1907: The Language of Flowers

The eloquent flower language is well understood by lovers when they are "talking sentiment" one to another. Each blossom is a letter in this alphabet. When grouped together or prettily clustered they spell—at least to lovers' understanding—the *soft, sweet nonsense* which to lovers' way of thinking is the wisest sense in the world.

For instance, a man may tastefully arrange a handful of pansies around a fragrant full-blown white rose and then add to his posy a moss rosebud. To the lady receiving these flowers the pansies will say, "You occupy my thoughts"; the white rose, "I am worthy of you"; the moss rosebud, "I now confess my love." If the lady is willing to encourage her lover to speak more plainly, she may send him a bunch of daisies. Wild daisies will tell him, "I will think of it," but garden daisies, grown less shy, will say, "I share your sentiments."

—New York Society of Self-Culture, *Correct Social Usage*

Chapter Fifteen

Rules of Engagement

Q Dear Miss Abigail:

I really can't live without her! I'm about to pop the question. Is it still necessary to ask the bride-to-be's father for his approval?

A It is hardly mandatory, but some young men do continue to follow the rules of simpler times and ask the father for his daughter's hand in marriage. I found some thoughts on engagement for you in John A. Ruth's etiquette book *Decorum*. Good luck with your proposal, and extra good luck with Papa (if you decide to go that route)! I'm rooting for you.

1880: Proposal of Marriage

The mode in which the avowal of love should be made must, of course, depend upon circumstances. It would be impossible to indicate the style in which the matter should be told. The heart and the head—the best and truest partners—

the utmost care should be taken

suggest the most proper fashion. Station, power, talent, wealth, complexion; all have much to do with the matter; they must all be taken into consideration in a formal request for a lady's hand. If the communication be made by letter, the utmost care should be taken that the proposal be clearly, simply, and honestly stated. Every allusion to the lady should be made with marked respect. Let it, however, be taken as a rule that an interview is best; but let it be remembered that all rules have exceptions.

ASKING PAPA. When a gentleman is accepted by the lady of his choice, the next thing in order is to go at once to her parents for their approval. In presenting his suit to them he should remember that it is not from the sentimental but the practical side that they will regard the affair. Therefore, after describing the state of his affections in as calm a manner as possible, and perhaps hinting that their daughter is not indifferent to him, let him at once frankly, without waiting to be questioned, give an account of his pecuniary resources and his general prospects in life, in order that the parents may judge whether he can properly provide for a wife and possible family. A pertinent anecdote was recently going the rounds of the newspapers. A father asked a young man who had applied to him for his daughter's hand how much property he had. "None," he replied, but he was "chock full of days' work." The anecdote concluded by saying that he got the girl. And we believe all sensible fathers would sooner bestow their daughters upon industrious, energetic young men who are not afraid of days' work than upon idle loungers with a fortune at their command.

—John A. Ruth, *Decorum: A Practical Treatise on Etiquette and Dress of the Best American Society*

1888: Engagement

When a gentleman feels that his relations with the lady he admires are such as to warrant his making an offer of marriage to her, it is more manly and straightforward for him to make the proposal verbally, than in writing.

—Elisabeth Marbury, *Manners: A Handbook of Social Customs*

1922: The Ring

The ring is given by the man immediately after the announcement of the engagement to the woman, who wears it on the third finger of her left hand. It should be a small and unostentatious one. Diamonds, rubies, moonstones, sapphires, and other precious stones may be used.

He may ask the woman to aid him in the selection, but it is better for him to make the selection alone. The woman may give the man an engagement ring or a gift if she wishes.

—W. C. Green, *The Book of Good Manners: A Guide to Polite Usage for All Social Functions*

Perhaps you find yourself in a situation where your guy has been a little timid about popping the question. After all, once you set the mood for romance, how could he *not* ask you to be his darling wife? Helen Andelin, in her book *The Fascinating Girl,* suggests:

1970: Securing Action

Few men propose in a mood of cold and calculating reason. The girl should endeavor, therefore, to arouse in him the opposite moods—a feeling of warm, impulsive emotion, or of *dreamy, drifting surrender to sentiment*. In such a mood, reason is subdued and the impulse to speak out is unopposed. The manner of awakening these sentimental moods is accompanied by *creating romantic situations.* A number of suggestions are given here.

A COZY WINTER EVENING: The atmosphere can be even more suggestive of sentiment if it is winter and the wind is howling outside and sleet is dashing against the window. How cozy and comforting it is for the girl and the boy, sitting before an open fire with the lights dimmed, to sit and dream. The man may feel that he would like for this to continue forever. There cannot be obstacles, he feels, when life is as easy and peaceful as this. How easy for him to succumb to his desire and forget his fears.

WATER: LAKES, RIVERS, THE OCEAN: Even in broad daylight, the effect of water is often spellbinding, especially upon those who may live daily in a crowded city. Night, water, and romance are inseparable. Have you ever noticed how young people are inclined to spend their vacations or holidays on or near water? There is a reason. Nothing is more soothing, more calculated to subdue fears and draw a man or woman close to each other than a night scene on the water, with the moon and stars shining on the ripples, the gentle lap of waves upon a beach or against a boat, and the mysterious blackness of a distant shoreline. Many men have innocently taken a girl on a boating excursion at night and returned to find themselves engaged.

PARKS AND GARDENS: A stroll through some beautiful garden, or in the hills or mountains, or in the woods, can often superinduce the atmosphere desired. There is nothing like getting back to nature to encourage a man to follow nature's impulse to take a mate for himself.

—Helen B. Andelin, *The Fascinating Girl*

Anyone up for a research project? I personally am hoping the odds have changed since the following was written in 1878.

1878: Who Live Longer?

Marry or die

Who live longer? The married or the celibate?

The answer is the same, seek it in the statistics of what country you will. In France, in England, in Scotland, in the United States, there are, in proportion to their respective number, more than twice as many married men still living at the age of seventy, as single (more exactly 26.9 married to 11.7 unmarried . . .). This is alarming odds against the bachelors. Well might the registrar of Scotland say that it almost means, "Marry or die."

—George H. Napheys, *The Transmission of Life: Counsels on the Nature and Hygiene of the Masculine Function*

Assuming that the proposal was a success, we now turn to the etiquette of engaged persons. All eyes will be on you as you prepare for the wedding of your dreams, so that means one thing: better behave!

1922: Courtship Courtesies

Once a man and girl are definitely engaged, certain courtship courtesies they owe each other are obvious. While no engaged man is dispensed from the proper social attentions due to other women, it is self-evident that he cannot pay any other woman too many attentions given the

fiancée, the bride-elect often receives his most intimate nature. In the same way, an engaged girl should avoid having her name coupled with that of any partiular man other than her intended, sit out dances with him, etc.

Then come the courtesies the engaged persons themselves owe society. In Baltimore and Philadelphia a chaperon is a society courtesy with which the engaged couple may dispense when going to theatre parties or dances. In Boston and New York, the chaperon is an essential. No engaged couple should ever take a journey which lasts overnight; nor should *fiancées* motor to roadhouses for meals unchaperoned. Society regards as discourteous the dining of engaged couples alone in restaurants, but condones their lunching or taking afternoon tea.

In general, though "all the world loves a lover," it does not appreciate a public display of happiness on his part. Courtship courtesy—even in these free and easy days—regards showing any amatory emotion in public as distinctly vulgar. Lovers, naturally, are supposed to kiss and cuddle—but not before others—for this is a courtship *discourtesy* which society at large justly resents. In general, courtship should and does bring out in every man the finest

the finest flower of his courtesy

flower of his courtesy and consideration. It is during courtship that he most desires to appear at his best in the eyes of the person to whom he is paying court. Too many lovers, alas, allow courtship courtesy to lapse after marriage, instead of continuing it as a lifelong habit.

—Harriet Lane, *The Book of Culture*

1929: Love Is a Species of Drunkenness

Romantic love is a species of drunkenness—even dullards are aware of this; they are aware of it when they are not in love, and either forget it or disregard it when they are.

Because of this drunkenness, it is never possible for two persons in love really to know one another; they only know what they think of one another.

Therefore all persons who marry for reasons of romantic love marry strangers; that is why marriage has been termed a lottery—and with justice.

marriage has been termed a lottery

It is true that marriage has nowadays ceased to be quite the lottery it formerly was, for at any rate some attempt is made on the part of young people to get really to know one another before they stand together at the altar. But even so, those who in the face of conventional morality permit themselves a certain amount of pre-conjugal intimacy, are only one degree (though an important one) nearer to safety than their more conventional brethren or fore-fathers. So long as engaged couples do not actually live together, in every sense of the word, in the same house, they may still, despite their intimacy, continue to remain in love, and hence fail to see each other as they really are.

This observation on my part, however, should not be miscon-
strued: a poet may have voiced the idea that as regards matrimony
the wisest and safest thing a man can do is to marry his mistress—
but it is not exactly my mission to uphold and disseminate such a
doctrine.

—·"A Husband" (Cyril Scott), *The Art of Making a*
Perfect Husband

1890: Engagements

such
excitements
are injurious

Long engagements are to be avoided, especially if the parties are frequently in each other's
society. There are good physiological reasons why the close relations
sustained by the lady and gentleman engaged should not be continued
for a very long time.

A certain degree of excitement of the sexual system is a necessary
consequence of the caresses and admiring glances which lovers bestow
upon each other. This is an excitement which meets with no gratification. All such excitements are injurious to the nervous system if they
occur frequently and are long continued . . . [especially to] those who
are very sensitive and easily excited.

Again, as a consequence of sexual desires being ungratified, in the
course of time indifference may spring up and the physical factor in
love may die for want of consummation.

—"An Old Practitioner" (G. Dallas Lind), *The Mother's*
Guide and Daughter's Friend.

Many of you engaged folk out there are probably secretly terrified at the prospect of spending the rest of your life with the same person. Those fears are perfectly normal, as you'll read in the next excerpt.

1963: Rational and Irrational Fears of Marriage

Let us not rashly assume that all fears of getting married are irrational or neurotic, for some aren't. As we have pointed out in the last two chapters, there are many real disadvantages of the marital state, and there is also a good chance that if you do wed you may easily pick the wrong girl. Consequently, there are some very good reasons for seriously considering, if not completely avoiding, marriage; and you *do* have some cause for fear in this connection.

You may, for example, truly be unable to afford marriage, and may logically have to put aside any idea of getting hitched for one or more years from now, when you may be in a much better financial condition. Or you may be too emotionally unbalanced, at the moment, to live together with any normal woman, and you may wish to go for therapeutic help, or otherwise to work out some of your emotional problems, before you attempt to do so. Or you may live in a small community where there is very little chance of your obtaining the kind of intelligent, cultured, stable girl whom you would like to marry, and you may decide to put off marrying for a time, until you go to reside in a larger community, where the marital choices might be much better.

Since, in general, marriage is a serious affair, and since it *may* be most inconvenient (and expensive!) for you to make a poor choice in the marriage you are contemplating, you should

be cautious about marrying

certainly, to say the least, be cautious about marrying and should not precipitately jump into the first fairly good relationship that presents itself.

—Albert Ellis, *Sex and the Single Man*

1890: Breaking Engagements

Should an engagement ever be broken? There are many who make a boast of the number of times they have been engaged. It is a dangerous amusement. Such persons

a dangerous amusement

often lose the ability to love anyone. There are, however, rare cases where a girl who has pledged herself to a man afterward sees him in a different light, and is convinced that she cannot be happy with him. It is then her duty to renounce him.

—"An Old Practitioner" (G. Dallas Lind), *The Mother's Guide and Daughter's Friend*

Chapter Sixteen
Here Comes the Bride

Q   Dear Miss Abigail:
Our wedding day is fast approaching! What advice can you
give us to help make it a perfect experience?

A   So much classic advice has been written on wedding etiquette that it would require a separate volume of excerpts to
get you up to speed on all of the details you are expected to
know. Rather than bore you with technicalities like who
travels down the aisle in what order, or what the role of the
bridesmaids should be, I'd like instead to share a few fun bits
of wedding advice from yesteryear. To put yourselves in the
mood, sing along with me now: "Here comes the bride . . .
all dressed in white. . . ."

1923: Wedding Preparations

As the engagement draws near an end, the young woman begins to turn her attention more definitely to the subjects of a trousseau, the wedding, and the wedding journey. These matters rest very largely in her hands, and it is well, therefore, for her to give careful consideration to them. She will, of course, make her own decisions upon these matters, but a few words of advice may not be amiss.

While it is delightful to have a plentiful supply of all sorts of dainty wearing apparel when one marries, it is much more important to be in the best possible health and spirits. For this reason, it is not well for the bride-to-be to plan a great lot of hand-embroidered lingerie which will call forth the envy of her girl companions and probably the execration of her future unfortunate laundress. Daintiness and simplicity can go together, and some of her time and strength and eyesight might well be devoted to other and more important matters at this time. . . .

all sorts of dainty wearing apparel

As for the wedding, if she will consult her husband-to-be, she will find, in the majority of instances, that the one thing he is praying for fervently is to be allowed to have a simple, unostentatious wedding. Since the life they are entering upon together is still more or less of an experiment, it would seem to be in good taste for them to be rather modest about it. When they come to celebrate their silver or golden wedding anniversary, then they can afford to make a big splurge.

—Bernarr Macfadden, *Womanhood and Marriage*

1912: The Wedding Day

The wedding day is one that shall ever be remembered and held sacred among life's anniversaries. It is a day whose benediction should fall on all other days to the

make the occasion itself just as delightful as possible

end of life. It should stand out in the calendar bright with all the brightness of love and gratitude. The memory of the wedding hour in a happy marriage life should shine like a star, even in old age.

It is surely worthwhile, therefore, to make the occasion itself just as delightful as possible, to gather about it and into it whatever will help to make it memorable, so that it shall stand out bright and sacred among all life's days and hours. This is not done when the marriage is secret; there are no associations about the event in that case to make its memory a source of pleasure in after years. Nor is it done when, on the other hand, the occasion is made one of great levity or of revelry; the joy of marriage is not hilarious, but deep and quiet.

On the wedding day the happy pair should have about them their

true friends, those whom they desire to hold in close relations in their after life. It is not time for insincerity; it is no place for empty professions of friendship. Everything about the circumstances—the festivities, the formalities, the marriage ceremony itself, the congratulations—should be so ordered as to cause no jar, no confusion, nothing to mar the perfect pleasure of the occasion, and so as to leave only the pleasantest memory behind.

These may seem too insignificant matters for mention here, yet it is surely worthwhile to make the occasion of one's wedding such that it shall always be remembered with a thrill of delight, with only happy associations and without one smallest incident or feature to mar the perfections of its memory.

—J. R. Miller, *The Wedded Life*

1923: The Wedding Dress

Today the keynote of the wedding gown is simplicity. The days of elaborate gowns with trains so heavy with the weight of precious jewels that eight girls had to carry them, is over. The sensible American bride knows that simplicity is more becoming to the solemn dignity of the occasion than extremely elaborate dress. . . .

so heavy with the weight of precious jewels

From a study of the descriptions of other bridal gowns at recent important weddings, we find that the satin is without doubt the favorite material. Crêpe-de-chine and heavy white brocade are also used; and the bride may select whichever material she likes best, something soft and clinging unless she is inclined to be too slender, when taffeta is more suitable. Undoubtedly, no matter what the style of the gown happens to be, it should boast a train, and a draped skirt is always a popular wedding mode. The length of the sleeves and skirt is entirely governed by the fashion of the moment.

White satin slippers and white gloves enhance the simple beauty of the wedding gown. Jewels are rarely worn, except, perhaps, one large gem—a gift of the groom.

—Lillian Eichler, *Book of Etiquette*

While this wasn't written expressly for brides, I think a bit of shoe advice is appropriate for your wedding day. After all, you're going to be on your feet for a majority of the day, and it's my bet you don't want to be thinking about corns, bunions, or a tottering gait when you're walking down the aisle.

1840: Tightness in Shoes

Ladies are very apt to torture their feet, to make them appear very small. This is exceedingly ridiculous: a very small foot is a deformity. True beauty of each part consists in the proportion it bears to the rest of the body.

A tight or ill-made shoe not only destroys the shape of the foot, it produces corns and bunions; and it tends to impede the circulation of the blood. Besides, the foot then swells and appears larger than it is, and the ankles become thick and clumsy.

The pernicious effect of tight or ill-made shoes is evident also in the still and tottering gait of these victims of a foolish prejudice: they can neither stand upright, walk straight, nor enter a room properly.

To be too short is one of the greatest defects a shoe can have, because it takes away all chance of yielding in that direction, and offering any compensation for tightness in others, and, in itself, it not only causes

the still and tottering gait of these victims

pain and spoils the shape of the foot by turning down the toes and swelling up the instep, but is the cause of bad gait and carriage.

—Mrs. A. Walker, *Female Beauty, as Preserved and Improved by Regimen, Cleanliness and Dress*

The following superstitions were published in a small pamphlet called "Dream Book Bridal Superstitions" by Dr. Ray Vaughn Pierce, president of the Invalids Hotel in Buffalo, New York. I'm not sure what dreams and bridal superstitions had to do with selling his quack medicines, which were named "Dr. Pierce's Favorite Prescription," "Dr. Pierce's Pleasant Pellets," "Dr. Pierce's Salve," and the like, but based on the testimonies printed in this booklet, they must somehow have enticed homemakers to order his drugs. Now, would you please pass the Pleasant Pellets?

1895: Here Comes the Bride: Old-Time Bridal Superstitions

On no account should a bride or a bridegroom be handed a telegram on the way to church.

The bride must be careful when leaving the church to put her right foot first. It is deemed most unfortunate for a bride to make the first step into the new world with the left foot.

put her right foot first

To have an unequal number of guests at the wedding breakfast or supper is unlucky.

If one of the bridesmaids immediately pours a kettle of hot water on the front doorstep as the newly married couple leave the house for their honeymoon, there will, within twelve months, be another wedding in the group.

—V. M. Pierce, *Dream Book Bridal Superstitions*

1888: Wedding Presents

It is customary for the relatives and friends of the bride and groom to send presents to the former before the wedding day. A card of the donor should accompany the gift. Presents are usually shown at the wedding reception. Sometimes the cards of the donors are left attached to the presents, but it is rapidly becoming the fashion to take them off. The bride should never neglect to write a note of thanks, or to personally thank the friends who have kindly remembered her through their gifts.

never neglect to write a note of thanks

—Elisabeth Marbury, *Manners: A Handbook of Social Customs*

Brides and grooms beware: it's often during the planning and execution of the wedding ceremony that reality sets in. Not only are you marrying your true love, you're marrying the entire family! No matter what your outrageous mother-in-law wears, or what your father-in-law with, ahem, "different" political views says, you know what? I'm betting you're never going to change them. So take a deep breath and relax, and try to enjoy them as much as you can. This won't necessarily teach you how to do that, but I found it entertaining anyway.

1956: In-Laws

One of the things that in any microscopic study of In-Laws is too often forgotten is that In-Laws are people! In plainer language—in order to get to be In-Laws themselves, however unlikely it seems, they

In-Laws are people!

had to have In-Laws! Furthermore, their In-Laws' In-Laws had to have In-Laws. The mathematical progression principle applied to this produces staggering results. Viz.: It takes four In-Laws to produce one married person; thus there are, at a given period in your married life— say when you're around thirty—perhaps eight times as many In-Laws in the world as there are married couples—not counting step-In-Laws.

—Emily Hahn and Eric Hatch, *Spousery*

Chapter Seventeen

Dream Honeymoon

Q Dear Miss Abigail:

Our dream honeymoon has been planned. Still, I'm a little nervous about traveling with my new spouse. What should I expect?

A How exciting! Your very first trip as husband and wife. I'm assuming you've chosen someplace you'll both enjoy, and have scheduled plenty of time to relax and recover from your wedding. I've compiled some notes on the subject of the honeymoon just for the occasion.

1904: The Honeymoon

Let the newly married couple take a holiday, the longer the better, and enjoy together the beauties of Nature, and all that they can command of the treasures of art, music, and literature; let them read together, and discuss what they read. Through the activity of the intellect the other faculties are developed and harmonized, and the affections cemented; and the long lovers' rides, walks, and talks thus store up treasures, not only in the memory, but in health and happiness, welding the two lives more perfectly into one harmonious whole.

Perfect freedom from business and all other cares is required for the real enjoyment of the honeymoon. During the sacred season of the first wedded privacy, the bride and groom do well to go away, and if possible spend it where curious neighbors, critical relatives, or extremes of heat or cold will not add discomfort to the delicately trying situation of the new relationship. With the most favorable conditions, it will still be no slight task, for two persons accustomed to seeing each other well dressed, to prevent a slight feeling of disillusionment when the negligee is first donned in each other's presence; when the curl-papers are in evidence and the quoting of poetry is possibly replaced by, or mingled with, the sewing on of buttons. It requires time to learn to regard these little daily intimacies as a matter of course; but with love as a foundation, they soon come to seem natural, and grow more dear as the months and years pass.

perfect freedom from business and all other cares

—Mary Ries Melendy, *Vivilore: The Pathway to Mental and Physical Perfection*

Traveling by plane to your honeymoon destination? This, written in 1924 by one of my favorite etiquette advisors, Lillian Eichler, offers up some helpful advice about air travel. Now, I don't know much about the design of early airplanes, but I'm so glad times have changed. Can you imagine passengers today attempting to toss trash out of a jet while airborne? Oh, my.

1924: In Flight

On most of the large planes, passengers are given glassine envelopes containing cotton and chewing gum. The experienced traveler pads his ears with the cotton and chews the gum to adjust his ears and throat to higher altitude. This is one occasion when chewing gum is not frowned upon as a vulgarity!

While the plane is aloft, passengers may get up and move about—if they like—but they must not venture into parts of the plane where it is forbidden to go. For example, the pilots' compartment is strictly tabu to passengers. So also is the mail and express compartment, which, on many planes, is directly behind the passenger cabin. Radio instruments and controls are usually located inside the pilots' compartment, but sometimes space is given inside the cabin to a special radio room. Passengers must not enter this room nor touch any of the instruments

Passengers should not drop paper, matches, or anything else out of a plane. Such things should be given to the cabin attendant to dispose of.

strangers are drawn to each other by the common thrill

The cabin of a plane is so small, the passengers in such close proximity, that any attempt to observe social formalities is quite out of the question. Nobody waits to be introduced —everybody talks to everybody else—strangers are drawn to each other by the common thrill of flying (it's still new enough to be thrilling to most of us!). . . .

It is not customary to tip airplane hostesses. However, if a hostess has been especially kind and attentive and the passenger wishes to show his appreciation, he may have a small, impersonal gift such as a box of candy or an interesting new book mailed to her after the trip is over.

—Lillian Eichler, *Etiquette in Public*

1963: The Best Travelers

The best travelers are:

- Open-minded—they love new places, new friends, new experiences.
- Self-reliant—they know at least roughly how to get where they

are going; they cope tearlessly with little travel tragedies, such as late arrivals and misplaced luggage.

- Organized—they can always find their tickets; they look neat, and so do their suitcases.

cope tearlessly with little travel tragedies

- Considerate—they are quiet; they don't spread their belongings about on train seats which aren't theirs; they don't leave a trail of litter behind them.

- Comfortably dressed—in wrinkle-resisting, easy-fitting clothes, in colors and patterns that don't show smudges readily. They have a sweater handy for extra warmth, a raincoat that doubles as a topcoat. They wear shoes intended to be *walked* in.

- Pleasing to the eye—on buses, planes, and trains, they dress tastefully, conservatively. Girls forego shorts or slacks in favor of a skirt; they choose an easy, wrinkle-resistant skirt when a long ride on a plane or sit-up train is in prospect. Young travelers of both sexes are prepared for social emergencies: a boy has a tie, a girl has some form of head covering—a scarf, net bonnet, packable hat—for quick compliance with the custom of a restaurant, a concert, a church, an unexpected party.

—Enid A. Haupt, *The Seventeen Book of Etiquette & Entertaining*

Now for the *really* important part of your honeymoon. Experiencing "married love"—the joining of husband and wife for the very, very, very first time (ahem)! Here are some excerpts to help ease your mind about the big night. The first is from a fabulous book titled *Bed Manners and Better Bed Manners*. The cover claims that the book will tell you "how to bring sunshine into your nights," and professes to have "many devilish illustrations" (too bad you can't see them all). Now you kids have some fun!

1940: How to Invite Somebody to Bed

You "date yourself" far more by what you say than by the way you look. The use of worn-out language (especially slanguage) is fatal to the best efforts of your barber and tailor, your gymnasium instructor, and all the others who try to make you seem youthful and sprightly. And if you're a lady—why, you may spend your allowance ten times over at the modiste's and

the beauty parlor, and still be recognized for a grandmother if you use a grandmother's wisecracks.

If you say: "Let us retire!" you date from the 1870s.

If you say: "Let's hit the hay!" you date from the 1880s.

If you say: "How about pounding your ear?" or speak of your bed as "the feathers," you are using slang of nearly as ancient vintage. To speak of going to bed as "flopping" is also not very new. In fact there is nothing safer and more modern to say than "Let's go to bed."

But people do get tired of saying this over and over again, especially if they have to say it several times every evening, before good results are attained. Comical bishops in English novels usually vary it by making up a phrase such as "Let's all go to Bedfordshire!" But this also is old.

To be thought young and dashing you need a wholly new piece of slang. It is always piquant to make it up yourself, and not depend on seeing it in the newspaper, or overhearing it at a party. Here is the way to proceed:

It was funny to call a bed "the hay" for a few years after the mattress was stuffed with hay. But your mattress is now stuffed with selected South American horsehair, full of correctly tempered hourglass springs, and magically insulated with fleecy felt. If you don't believe us, cut it open. Or read the advertisement of that mattress.

You would surprise and perhaps charm almost anybody, even your husband, if instead of saying "Let's hit the hay!" you said: "Let's hit the selected South American horsehair, full of correctly tempered hourglass springs, etc., etc." But maybe this is too long to learn by heart—and it certainly won't sound funny twice.

What you need, to refresh your way of speaking, are some good, reliable words that mean "bed." A short list includes bunk, berth, pallet, crib, cot, shakedown, *lit* (French) and *palang* (Hindu). Then you want a few good words that mean "lie down," "yawn," "snore," "take a rest," and so forth. You might trust the dictionary, but never trust a dictionary too far. Or you will find yourself saying to some startled person, who never went to school in Boston, something that he or she won't understand.

Shall we oscitate in our palang?

Only if your wife was a Boston girl can you say:

"I am somniferous. Are you statuvolvent? Shall we oscitate in our palang?"

It is really simpler to say: "Let's go to bed."

—Ralph Y. Hopton and Anne Balliol, *Bed Manners and Better Bed Manners*

If you're having any trouble at all with the "marital act," there is a plethora of advice books out there to help. One such is C. B. S. Evans's *Man and Woman in Marriage*—"a sound, comprehensive statement of normal sex problems and sex relations . . . a detailed exposition of the perfect expression of physical love." After reading this, I'm sure you'll be ready for anything.

1931: Intercourse

In looking back over the history of sex in marriage, one discovers that, from time to time, there have been changes in the fashion of having intercourse. Today we have quite generally adopted a particular variety of the prone position which was not the vogue centuries ago. It is difficult to analyze the forces which have swayed whole nations into the popular belief that any particular method was the only correct or proper one.

making it as satisfactory to one as to the other

A position should be selected which will be perfect for both man and wife. It cannot be expected that any one method will prove satisfactory to both. A man can buy a ready-made suit that will fit himself; a woman, a ready-made dress that will meet her requirements. How many can buy a ready-made garment, for instance, pyjamas, that will fit them both? A married couple should make-to-order their own particular position, building it upon definite principles, with the end in view of making it as satisfactory to one as to the other.

—C. B. S. Evans, *Man and Woman in Marriage*

1942: Laugh Away Awkwardness

have a great deal of fun

Things go a bit awkwardly at first— naturally one must become accustomed to thinking and planning in certain ways. But after a *few repetitions* your actions become automatic, which is what we really mean when we say "natural." And you really can have a great deal of fun. When you are awkward, laugh at yourself. Few of us laugh enough.

—Margery Wilson, *The Woman You Want to Be*

Chapter Eighteen

Making Your House a Home

Q Dear Miss Abigail:

We want to make our new home special. What suggestions do you have for settling into our new life together?

A Whether you decide to buy a house or rent an apartment together, setting up your first home as a couple can be a wonderful experience. With paint colors to select, furniture to arrange, shiny new pots and pans to put away, and cleaning schedules to plan, you'll be busy in these first few months. But there is naturally more to your home than the things that are in it.

1904: Establishing the Home

Life and its chief inspiration, love, are made up of the blending of two elements—the spiritual and the phys- *weaving the beautiful threads of idealism* ical. The spiritual glorifies, while the physical sustains. In establishing family life, the rosy dreams of courtship and the honeymoon must have, not a rude, but a healthy awakening; for such a prominent part of the thoughts of both, and to keep up the poetry and charm of life under such circumstances will require something of the artist's skill in weaving the beautiful threads of idealism into the commonplace. Yet it can be done, and by remembering to include lovemaking as an indispensable part of the daily routine of homemaking, marriage can be kept from descending to the material plane, even in the midst of homely surroundings and prosaic tasks.

—Mary Ries Melendy, *Vivilore: The Pathway to Mental and Physical Perfection*

1902: Peace at Home

Peace at home, that is the boon. "He is the happiest, be he king or peasant, who finds peace in his home." Home should be made so truly home that the weary tempted heart could turn toward it anywhere on the dusty highway of life and receive light and strength; should be the sacred refuge of our lives, whether rich or poor. The ties that bind the wealthy and the proud to home may be forged on earth, but those which link the poor man to his humble hearth are of true metal and bear the stamp of heaven.

—Professor B. G. Jefferis, *The Household Guide, or Domestic Cyclopedia*

Double mattress?
　　　Twin size mattresses?
　Super size mattress?
　　　Innerspring or Foam?

Our Advice: *Talk it over with your husband-to-be...then choose what you both want in a* Sealy Posturepedic

Furnishing a double bedroom is a job for two people. He likes blue. You like green. So you do a blue and green color scheme, and everybody's happy.

But deciding on a mattress is different. You don't pick it for color, you pick it for comfort. Mutual comfort. And there's only one way to do it successfully. Go to your store *together*, and find exactly what you both want in a Sealy Posturepedic®.

The Posturepedic comes in every size, twin to foam construction. . . . the famous firm rincess. No matter is assurance: every peration with lead-n support. This not sleeping, it means eping on a too-soft eople as young as

sses or Matching $79.50.

d

your mattress

Advice to single girls
on furnishing a double bedroom.

turn the page. please

Here's a little something from one of my home economics books regarding the need for a place to rest, relax, and sleep comfortably. I hope you've been able to create this in your happy new home.

1947: Provision for Sleep and Peace

We spend long hours in bed and should arise rested, refreshed, and ready for the work and play of the day. We drop down in our favorite easy chair for a moment, and the

everyone is overstimulated

charm and restfulness of the orderly quiet room seem to restore something within us essential to satisfying living. The need for privacy is deep-seated in each of us. We need time by ourselves to think things through, to sort our impressions, and to reflect on our beliefs. In earlier years, when our population was largely rural, people found privacy in the woods and fields, as well as in their homes. Now, every moment of the day has potential contact with many people. Automobiles, telephones, and radios seem to eliminate distance, as artificial light has shortened the night. The result is that everyone is overstimulated. If we are to have opportunity for serenity and poise, the home must provide for us times and places for the enjoyment of the quiet that allows one to think, to read, to relax, and to plan. The rest that will rebuild one for the stress of the next day must be assured.

—Margaret Justin and Lucile Rust, *Today's Home Living*

1890: Sleeping Together

Many writers on sexual hygiene say that man and wife should not occupy the same bed. I see no physiological or moral reason why they should not. Of course a bedroom should be well ventilated. There should be air enough for two sets of lungs, and both parties should be clean and wear clean clothes. There are times when the parties should be continent and it may be difficult for some men and women to sleep in the same bed and be able to control their desires. If such is the case, then separate beds should be enjoined, but I think these cases are rare. . . . There is an advantage in man and wife sleeping together. The close companionship develops and sustains mutual love. . . . One of the greatest pleasures of the married state is certainly that of man and wife resting side by side after the toils of the day are over and in the quiet of the night.

resting side by side after the toils of the day

—"An Old Practitioner" (G. Dallas Lind), *The Mother's Guide and Daughter's Friend*

Cooking, cleaning, and ironing, oh my! The next few quotes are geared toward the "housewife" as she brings order to the new home. Now, don't get your hackles up, I know the wife-only notion of housekeeping is archaic. But that's just how it was back then, and so it's perpetuated in many of the classic advice books. Don't blame me! If you're really offended by this and would prefer a more contemporary take on things, mentally replace the "woman" with "man," the "wife" with "husband," or the "she" with "he" half the time. That should make you feel better.

1952: Homemaker or Housekeeper?

Homemaker or Housekeeper? Given a choice I'm sure there isn't a woman who would prefer to be called a housekeeper in preference to a homemaker! Yet, "to be a good homemaker, one must be a good house-keeper."

Homemaking today offers as much of a challenge to the modern woman as it did to her great-grand-mother! Today's new textiles, new electrical equipment, new foods, new homemaking techniques are things great-grandma never knew. But today's homemaker is expected to be "in the know" and up-to-date in her housekeeping, just because she is a modern woman.

as much of a challenge to the modern woman

What's more—she wants to be! But it isn't as easy as it sounds. There are so many new things to keep up with, so many sources supplying this information, and so little time for the busy homemaker to keep up-to-date! . . .

The schedule is the thing. You'll soon have a schedule if you "use your head to save your heels" as the book says. It's a wonderful suggestion for anyone. I'd like to add another and say "get off your feet and onto your seat" so you save your energy whenever possible! You'll be better company for your family if you are not physically exhausted. If these few suggestions are followed, I can guarantee from past experience you will be well on your way toward making your house into a home! And doing it the easy way, too! What more could a woman ask?

—Marjorie Roehl Kaschewski, *Housekeeping Made Simple*

1965: Cooking for Two

The honeymoon is over; the die is cast. You and you only stand between your husband's and your own starvation. Either you surrender to the can-opener method of cooking, to allow you more time at the beauty parlor, or you make up your mind to follow a more rewarding path.

You decide to learn to cook well, to experiment and master culinary techniques, and to set interesting and nourishing meals on an attractive table.

Feeding a husband successfully starts with feeding him the things he likes to eat, for a clever bride cooks to please her man. She goes out of her way to keep mealtimes pleasant and comfortable. She knows that experts say "happy mealtimes are as important to health as proper food." And whether the meal is served informally in the kitchen, at the dining table by candlelight, or on trays in the living room with soft background music, the surroundings should be neat, the atmosphere one of relaxation, and there should be some special touch—a single flower floating in a glass saucer, a colorful napkin tied in a knot, a pretty china figurine—just to remind your husband how lucky he is to have "caught" you.

a clever bride cooks to please her man

—Evelyn Enright and Ann Seranne, *Happy Living! A Guidebook for Brides*

1902: Golden Rules for the Kitchen

Without cleanliness and punctuality good cooking is impossible.

Leave nothing dirty; clean and clear as you go.

A time for everything and everything in time.

A good cook wastes nothing.

An hour lost in the morning has to be run after all day.

Haste without hurry saves worry, fuss, and flurry.

Stew boiled is stew spoiled.

Strong fire for roasting.

Clear fire for broiling.

Wash vegetables in three waters.

Boil fish quickly, meat slowly.

a good cook wastes nothing

—Professor B. G. Jefferis, *The Household Guide, or Domestic Cyclopedia*

1962: Use the Best While You Can!

What I am trying to tell you sweet housewives is that there is no one more important in your home than *you*! So don't save your good things for "tomorrow"—use them now. Life is so short—enjoy every day of it.

Get your good silver out and put it in your kitchen drawer and use it every day. Use your good dishes at least once a week, if not daily. There is no one who will ever come into your home who is more important and loved any more than your own family. They are the greatest!

If you could only read some of the letters that come to me saying such things as:

"Heloise, I never knew how much I loved my husband until he was gone. I ate off old dishes, saved my good silver for company (and none was as good as he) and covered my beautiful satin comforter (the one he gave me) when I should have used it so that the beautiful satin would show and he could see it! If I had it to do over . . . Tell the young ones to enjoy their families and use their good things."

So go get that pretty sugar bowl out and so what if you put a soap pad in it? At least you are enjoying it daily!

—Heloise, *Heloise's Housekeeping Hints*

So what if you put a soap pad in it?

The inscription in my copy of Marjorie Holmes's *I've Got to Talk to Somebody, God,* reads: "To my darling wife—to use when I'm not around, Christmas, 1969." This sounds lovely—until you read some of the section headings in the book: "The Other Woman" ("This woman is attracted to my husband, Lord, and I don't know whether to be proud, amused, alarmed—or mad"); "The Quarrel" ("God, we quarreled again last night, and today my heart is sore"); "When a Husband Loses Interest" ("My husband has lost interest in me, Lord. I feel it. I know it"). But there is plenty of uplifting material in this book, too. I think I'll stick to a prayer about housekeeping. Think of this next time you're pressing your clothes.

1969: Prayer for Ironing

Dear God, as I iron these clothes for my family, please make me aware not what a chore it is, but what a blessing:

That we may have so many clothes to keep them warm. So many clothes to make them happy— pretty dresses, bright plaid shirts. Let me be thankful even for the trousers, hard as they are to press. Let me be thankful for having sons.

thank you for spray starch

Thank you for this iron, with its simple yet marvelous power—heat and steam.

Thank you for this sturdy ironing board. Thank you for spray starch, which has cut down my dampening time and makes everything so sweetly crisp. Thank you for this tumbled treasury of garments and tablecloths and pillow slips.

Thank you for the strength to make them smooth. And for all the hours of my life that I have been able to do this job, however I have dreaded it or put it off.

Give me the patience, please, to teach my own daughter this ancient art that every woman should know. And to teach my sons, as well, so that they, if they ever have to, can do their own.

And dear Lord, give me a spiritual strength to match this strength I bring to the smoothing of these clothes. As you have equipped my hands to guide this iron, please equip me with the wisdom to guide my children, to smooth out the wrinkles in their lives as well.

—Marjorie Holmes, *I've Got to Talk to Somebody, God*

An important part of setting up a new home is the establishment of cleaning routines. Now that there are two of you, this should be easy as pie. But first, there's the question of a housekeeper's appropriate attire. The following is written for gals, but I don't see any problem with hubby throwing on a nice little housedress before picking up the mop. I mean, it *is* your house. You can do whatever you want!

1929: Dressing to Your Part

Now there is another important phase to the business of being a housewife, and this you must never allow yourself to overlook. It is that of dressing to your part. You would not go to the office or to school in your oldest and shabbiest dress, would you? Then why do you think you should do your housework in it? In these hectic days the clever woman will look her best at all times for her husband and her children.

always a fresh apron in the offing

In the first place, your housedresses can be entirely practical, eminently suited to the purpose to which they will be put, and at the same time be attractive and becoming. There is absolutely no reason why they should be shapeless, ugly-looking affairs masquerading under the title of practicality. For if they are ugly they are decidedly impractical and extremely expensive in their psychological effects upon yourself as well as upon your family. Practicality is merely a matter of colors and materials that you can launder often and well and lines that do not hamper your working. These colors and materials can be becoming to you, and these lines can be modish. . . .

Getting breakfast isn't such a messy job, the way we do it! Therefore you can wear a pretty negligee for it. Then whisk into your yesterday's and perhaps not so very fresh housedress for the dishwashing—but with always a fresh apron in the offing to slip on when the doorbell rings. After your truly dirtiest work is done put on a fresh and slightly more elaborate dress, perhaps, for your marketing and for luncheon. And this, with the proper kind of apron, should survive the rest of the day until it is time to dress for dinner, something a lovely lady always does.

—Daré Frances, *Lovely Ladies: The Art of Being a Woman*

As you set about cleaning your house, you may wonder just how much clutter you can leave lying around before others consider your house dirty. *The Mother's Guide* offers this advice:

1890. What Is Dirt?

Anything which is offensive to the senses is dirt. Anything out of its proper place is dirt. The soil of the garden and the gravel of the street are not dirt in those situations, but they would be dirt on the floor of a house. Dust almost constantly on furniture may be unavoidable in some situations, as when the house is very close to a dusty street; but, as a general thing, to see dust thick enough to write your name in is an evidence of careless housekeeping. A whisk of a duster once a day or sometimes once in two days will keep furniture clean.

Some persons would regard books and papers on the floor, or carelessly strewn over a table, as dirt. If this be dirt it is, to say the least, a very pardonable kind. Persons who make but little use of books and papers usually keep them neatly arranged.

—"An Old Practitioner" (G. Dallas Lind), *The Mother's Guide and Daughter's Friend*

Okay, I know you're tired of pretending that all this housekeeping advice was written with woman *and men* in mind. Luckily, I've found this refreshing text by Margaret Sanger from 1940 which suggests that this is *not* all just woman's work.

1940: Household Duties

What were formerly considered exclusively feminine duties seem today to be voluntarily taken on by the husband. Surely there is no loss in manliness or dignity in sharing the heavier and more disagreeable household tasks. In my estimation this mutual acceptance of household duties by the husband as well as the wife does more than any other single thing toward the creation of that splendid comradeship and companionship which are the solidest foundations of permanent homes and happy marriages.

no loss in manliness

The husband who balks at such tasks and looks upon such duties as essentially feminine, who considers himself henpecked when asked to help in them, is indeed a pathetic creature. He is, moreover, exhibiting an ungenerous and thoughtless side of his nature which will be apprehensively watched by his wife. He cannot know the real joys of true companionship in his married life, and he has himself only to blame when his own action brings out similar traits in his wife. This has been the traditional and unfortunate attitude of many foreign-born men toward their wives. Women were not made merely to serve the physical and sexual needs of husbands, with no obligation on the part of the latter except to provide a house and to pay the bills. Fortunately for all of us this type of husband is fast becoming a thing of the past.

—Margaret Sanger, *Happiness in Marriage*

Chapter Nineteen

Getting Along as Husband and Wife

Q   Dear Miss Abigail:
The house is looking great. We've had a fantastic first few
months of marriage. But it has been a bit of an adjustment
getting used to having him around all the time. Sometimes
he makes me so crazy! Is this normal?

A   Ah, the honeymoon is over, as they say. As the dust settles
and newlyweds get used to living together, it's not
uncommon for some bumps along the road to a long
marriage to trip the couple up. Tom McGinnis has some
appropriate advice for you, from his book *Your First Year of
Marriage*. You might even want to pick up a copy, if this
chapter doesn't help.

1967: The Impact of Reality

Amid the joy, excitement, and sense of freedom and power you will experience in setting up your own home, you almost certainly will encounter some disillusionment. Its intensity will probably depend largely upon how closely your expectations about your mate and marriage have approximated reality.

There is some disenchantment in every marriage —a comedown from the bliss, glamour, and all-encompassing interest in each other that is characteristic of the first days. That a return to reality is inevitable is probably recognized by everyone. The phrase "The honeymoon is over" puts this recognition into language. . . .

a return to reality is inevitable

When the disenchantments and disillusionments of marriage are stretched out over a period of time, they are relatively easy to adjust to. Often, however, they appear all at once in a way that seems intolerable. Newlyweds often experience what might truly be described as a rude awakening—a condition in which the husband and wife may wonder, "What could have possessed me to marry this person? I must have been out of my mind." If the shock is too great, some persons never survive it, and their marriage is doomed from that point onward. Most people, however, come to realize that their expectations were unrealistic in the first place.

Along with the discovery of these new responsibilities comes the realization that the good times you enjoyed in each other's company before marriage now have to be replaced by good times to be enjoyed in a different way. During your dating days, courtship, and honeymoon, you saw your partner primarily as a recreational companion.

You learned how you act in each other's company when free of responsibility, when you have gone dancing together, attended parties, gone bowling, swimming, or riding, and so on. Courtship was relatively free of the pressures of living, a time for holding hands and whispering sweet compliments. Suddenly, it seems, you find yourself working around the house, disturbed by the need to prepare for meals, clean the oven, put up storm windows, sweep the rugs, or repair the faucets.

—Tom McGinnis, *Your First Year of Marriage*

This curious book presents two sides to the issue of "spousery": one for the wives and one for the husbands. On the "HER" side, the flap copy reads: "Men, turn this book over: Only a double book can do justice to the bi-sided subject of SPOUSERY. Women *only* may read this half of the book, and for *you*, madam, the price is

$2.98. A husband may flip this book over and read Emily Hahn on male SPOUSERY. . . . He will pay $3.00. We know men: they continue to ignore the pennies." On the "HIS." side, the instructions are the same, but end with: "She will pay $2.98: a bargain. (You see how well *we* understand women.)"

1896: How Do Couples Live Together?

If a man and a woman are to live together well, they must take the plant of love to the sunniest and securest place in their habitation. They must water it with tears of repentance, or tears of joy; they must jealously remove the destroying insects, and pluck off the dead leaves, that the living may take their place. And if they think they have any business in this life more pressing than the care and culture of the plant, they are undeserving of one another, and time's revenges will be swift and stern. Their love vows will echo in their lives like perjuries; the sight of their love letters in a forgotten drawer will affect them with shame and scorn; in the bitterness of their own disappointment they will charge God foolishly, and think that every plant of love has a worm at the root because they neglected theirs, and every married life is wretched because they did not deserve happiness.

take the plant of love to the sunniest and securest place

A man must give his mind to a wife, and a wife must give her mind to a husband, as well as the heart, if they are to make a success of it.

—Robert F. Horton, *On the Art of Living Together*

The young wife may be wondering how best to deal with the reality of having a man around the house. To explore some of the issues surrounding this question, I turn to J. H. Kellogg's advice from 1886.

1886: What Are You Going to Do with Him or for Him?

You have found a husband, it is to be hoped, to your mind, and suited to you, and now the question is, What are you going to do with him or for him? In the first place, make him a

you can afford to be generous and liberal

pleasant, cheerful, tidy home. Take good care of him. Particularly, take good care of his stomach, by supplying him with pure, wholesome food. If you can keep his digestion good, you can rely upon his keeping his temper, unless he is an extraordinarily ill-tempered man. Be careful always to treat him well, and demand that he should treat you well. Treat him respectfully, and insist that he shall treat you respectfully in return. Respect his rights of conscience, and require him to respect yours as well. Humor him a little, especially if you are in the right, and he in the wrong. You can afford to be generous and liberal if you have the right on your side, as you will certainly come out ahead in the long run.

—J. H. Kellogg, *Plain Facts for Old and Young: Embracing the Natural History and Hygiene of Organic Life*

1942: A Man's Appearance

Perhaps your husband has poor taste in clothes. What if it is even lousy? Commenting on poor taste or carelessness in dress is useless, for most husbands resent criticisms of their clothes. Of course your objective is to make your husband more attractive and look important even if he is

only a little-shot, and quite naturally you make suggestions from time to time as to his wardrobe, which
suggestions fall on deaf ears, or bring forth a look
of contempt which indicates "What do you know

*above all do
not nag*

about it?' or mind your own business." What you want to know is
what to do in case your husband
ignores or resents your suggestions. Above all do not nag, and
never say, "*Why* don't you ever get
a blue double-breasted suit? John
Smith certainly looks well in his
gray suit." "I wish you would wear
some other color suit except
brown." "You look terrible in blue
suits." Use diplomacy, and if you
want him to have a blue double-
breasted suit, say: "John, I think
a blue double-breasted suit would
be becoming to you." Naturally he

will want to know your reasons and will probably ask you "why?"

This is where the catch comes in, and really allows you to strut your
stuff. Use your head and instead of saying, "Because I like blue—I'm
sick of seeing you wear brown all the time," or similar remarks, say:
"Because a blue double-breasted suit would complement your profile,
tan complexion, eyes, shoulders, etc." He may say it is the bunk,
bologna, or accuse you of trying to kid him, but don't worry; men are
vain, too, and even if it is so much soft soap, they like it!

By using this approach, you are not only implanting the idea of his getting a suit you like, but of building up his ego by complimenting him on some favorable characteristic.

—J. Joseph Marshall, *Living with a Husband and Liking It*

Many young marrieds wonder how much and what sort of criticism of their spouse is acceptable—if any. No one wants to be a nag. Here's a little something about the topic:

1916: Shall Husbands and Wives Criticize?

It is a duty we owe to our friends, and especially to our best of all earthly friends—our wife or husband—to remind them, in a spirit of kindness and charity, of their faults, with a view to their correction. We must not do this in a censorious and self-righteous spirit, but considerately and tenderly, and we must not manifest impatience if the habits of years are not wholly abandoned in a week.

in a spirit of kindness and charity, of their faults

—Professor T. W. Shannon, *Nature's Secrets Revealed: Scientific Knowledge of the Laws of Sex Life and Heredity, or Eugenics*

1929: Most Women Are Born Actresses

Most women are born actresses by nature, but good women act in a good cause; they can heroically conceal sorrow beneath smiles, and self-sacrifice beneath

good women act in a good cause

flippancy. Therefore the husband who chafes at having to put up with his wife's faults should remember that in all probability his own are equally being put up with by her—but in such skilful wise that he is quite oblivious of the process.

—"A Husband" (Cyril Scott), *The Art of Making a Perfect Husband*

1947: Dangers to Marital Happiness

Another source of irritation is the tendency of married people to take each other increasingly for granted when the honeymoon is over. The pretty girl who took so much pride in her appearance during the days of courtship becomes careless. She grows indifferent about her diet, eats fats and sweets without any discipline, until she has developed the proportions of a barrel, and then begins to wonder why she fails to attract her husband. Within the house she disports herself in loose wrappers and baggy clothes, with her hair in disarray—a sight to make any man eager to leave the house early and return late. The husband, on the other hand, may regard his home as a kind of kennel or stable, where he can walk around in his stocking feet and bawl out orders or complaints with no regard for the amenities of civilized living.

This is not to assume that it is possible for all persons to be models of beauty or to retain sylphlike figures and employ at all times the exquisite manners and formalities of a courtier. Advancing years take their toll on the charms of youth; and within the home, both man and wife are entitled to a reasonable measure of informal comfort. Still, a thoughtful consideration of one's appearance and domestic manners can contribute much to tranquility and enduring respect. . . .

The considerate husband will keep in mind that his wife is a living, throbbing human being, not merely a galley slave to do his bidding. He will remember anniversaries, bring

his wife is a living, throbbing human being

home candy and flowers occasionally, and take his wife out to dinner and the theater. He will notice and praise her hats and clothes and tell her how beautiful she looks, not take these things for granted or make her feel simply extravagant or ridiculous.

Upon leaving for work and on his return he will kiss his wife, and not rush out and in like one who has no obligations of affection. He will frequently take his wife in his arms, as he did in days of courtship, and tell her that he loves her, and that she will always be the woman of his dreams. In a word, the happiness and loveliness of his wife will always be his chief concern, as he desires that she shall devote her life as a living flame to enkindle and illuminate his.

—Rev. James A. Magner, *The Art of Happy Marriage*

Chapter Twenty

And They Lived Happily
Ever After . . .

Q
Dear Miss Abigail:
We've heard horror stories of couples that grow apart after only a few years of marriage. How do we prevent that from happening to us?

A
Look at you, all grown up and married to the one you love. I'm so proud of how far you've come! If you've read the wise words of the classic advice givers with care, you should do just fine and live a long and prosperous life together. To begin this final chapter, I offer some guidance from a book titled *Home and Health and Home Economics*. Filled with everything from housekeeping tips to recipes to directions on how to bandage up wounds, this book also contains timeless advice for a husband and wife that you might be able to put to use more than one hundred years later.

1880: How to Perpetuate the Honeymoon

Continue your courtship. Like causes produce like effects. Do not assume a right to neglect your companion more after marriage than you did before.

have no secrets that you keep from your companion

Have no secrets that you keep from your companion. A third party is always disturbing.

Once married, never open your mind to any change. If you keep the door of your purpose closed, evil or even desirable changes cannot make headway without your help.

Make the best of the inevitable. Persist in looking at and presenting the best side. Such is the subtle constitution of the human mind, that we believe what we will; also, what we frequently tell.

Keep step in mental development. A tree that grows for forty years may take all the sunlight from a tree that stops growing at twenty.

Gauge your expenses by your revenues. Love must eat. The sheriff often levies on Cupid long before he takes away the old furniture.

Start from where your parents started rather than from where they are now. Hollow and showy boarding often furnishes the too strong temptation, while the quietness of a humble home would cement the hearts beyond risk.

Avoid debt. Spend your own money; then it will not be necessary to blame anyone for spending other people's.

Do not both get angry at the same time. It takes two to quarrel.

Do not allow yourself ever to come to an open rupture. Things un-said need less repentance.

Study to understand your companion's disposition, in order to please and avoid friction.

Study to confirm your tastes and habits to the tastes and habits of your companion. If two walk together, they must agree.

Chang and Eng were the Siamese Twins. Chang made Eng lie down
when sick. It killed Eng, and Chang could not survive
him. Take care of Eng. Few people survive divorce.

—C. H. Fowler and W. H. De Puy. *Home and*
Health and Home Economics

take care
of Eng

When I first read this excerpt from Edward Podolsky's *Sex Today in*
Wedded Life, I was reminded how lucky we are to be living today and
not in some earlier time. The lists suggest that the wife has a lot more
serious things to worry about than her husband, who only has to
remember her birthday and to kiss her in public. But then I noticed
some charming points. Read number ten in the wives' commandments
very carefully—let him *think* he wears the pants?

1947: Ten Commandments for Wives

1. Don't bother your husband with petty troubles and complaints
    when he comes home from work.

2. Be a good listener. Let him tell you his troubles; yours will
    seem trivial in comparison.

3. Remember your most important job is to build up and main-
    tain his ego (which gets bruised plenty in business). Morale is a
    woman's business.

4. Let him relax before dinner, and discuss family problems after
    the "inner man" has been satisfied.

5. Always remember he's a male and marital relations promote
    harmony. Have sane views about sex.

6. No man likes a wife who is always tired out. Conserve your
    energy so you can give him the companionship he craves.

7. Never hold up your husband to ridicule in the presence of others. If you must criticize, do so privately and without anger.

8. Remember a man is only a grown-up boy. He needs mothering and enjoys it if not piled on too thick.

9. Don't live beyond your means, or add to your husband's financial burdens.

10. Don't try to boss him around. Let him think he wears the pants.

Ten Commandments for Husbands

1. Remember your wife wants to be treated as your sweetheart always.

2. Remember her birthdays and your wedding anniversaries.

3. Bring her some gift every week, no matter how inexpensive it may be. (It's not the price, it's the thought.)

4. Don't take love for granted. Don't "ration" your kisses. Being a woman, she wants you to woo her.

5. Respect her privacy.

6. Always be tender, kind, and considerate even under trying circumstances.

7. Don't be stingy with money; be a generous provider.

8. Compliment her new dress, "hairdo," cooking, etc.

9. Always greet her with a kiss, especially when other people are around.

10. Remember marriage is a 50-50 proposition and you are not the majority stockholder.

—Edward Podolsky, *Sex Today in Wedded Life*

1940: The Husband as Lover

Happiness in marriage must be endlessly recaptured and renewed. It cannot be gained once and held forever in the possession of the husband. Therefore to husbands of all ages—young, middle-aged, and even old—these directions are indispensable: Keep on wooing.

Make the love you have found and which means so much to both of you *your religion*. For it can be the noblest of religions.

Keep your wife eternally youthful. This may seem an impossible task, but it is not and will more than repay you. Happiness is essential for the health and growth of love. Love must keep on growing. It cannot stand still. It grows or it dies. Love cannot thrive in silence. Therefore assure her, reassure her of your deep and growing affection. Good tidings invigorate the flagging energies of a band of explorers; a deep joy enables men and women to transcend the frail-ties of human weakness. Disappointment, sorrow depress and disturb the vital functions. Therefore, husband and wife as well, *tell your love* at all times to each other.

Some men only do this occasionally, or when desire is at high tide. They make a grave mistake. Acts may express this love more eloquently than words. But do not, on this account, conclude that words are not necessary also. They are. Love needs constant reassurance. Your wife is in all probability not a mind reader. Unless you tell her, break through the reticence and

keep on wooing

embarrassment of expressing your thoughts, she may never know what you are thinking and feeling.

This is a greater problem among men who are naturally taciturn and silent, among men who are born and brought up in a tradition which encourages a suppression of stirred emotions. But do not make the mistake of supposing that women do not like to be told over and over again of the love she inspires. This is a story women never tire of hearing. This is a thought all husbands should keep constantly in mind. This is the tonic that rejuvenates and keeps both young.

—Margaret Sanger, *Happiness in Marriage*

1915: Giving Love

In all aspects of personal relationship, giving is more important than receiving. To be loved is essential to our happiness: it is not necessary to the deepest life of the spirit. To that end, it is more important to love than to be loved. He who keeps sweet and sound, in his own breast, the capacity to love, can meet any disaster life may bring. He may be crushed down with pain, tortured with anguish; but if the activity of loving is unspoiled and strong in his heart, he may struggle to his feet and go on.

—Edward Howard Griggs, *Friendship, Love and Marriage*

With this final excerpt, my friends, I must bid you adieu and farewell. Your sendoff is a quote from Mary Ries Melendy's *Vivilore: The Pathway to Mental and Physical Perfection*. Here she speaks of what marriage is truly about.

1904: Not for Self, but for the Other

Love seeks to bless its object—is all the while endeavoring to minister to the loved one's delight—is a perpetual giver. True marriage consists in the complete consecration of each to the happiness of the other. Let each live not all for self, but for the other. Fancies, whims, caprices may seem foolish, but nevertheless it pays to indulge the loved one even in trifles. For a husband thus to gratify his wife in some wish, however slight, makes her inexpressibly happy because it is an added evidence of his love for her; and her own affection for him is thereby increased. The wife, also, who tries in little ways and in all ways to conform to her husband's preferences, finds in doing so her greatest delight. The unselfishness must be mutual. To those who resolve at the outset never to forget or neglect this law, and who keep their resolution, life will be a continual honeymoon.

—Mary Ries Melendy, *Vivilore: The Pathway to Mental and Physical Perfection*

Acknowledgments

This book wouldn't have come into being without the support and love of my family: Linda and Jim Salisbury; David Grotke; Rose Grotke; Chris Grotke; Lise LePage; Jennifer, Tony, Olivia, and Iris Perez; Deb, Lenn, Ally, and David Johns; and all my aunts, uncles, and cousins.

I am grateful to my editor, Johnny Saunders, for his enthusiasm and charm, and to Thunder's Mouth Press for believing in Miss Abigail. Thanks to my excerpt reviewers, readers, image hunters and scanners, and all-around hand-holders during the creation of this book, particularly Dad, Mom, Jim, Chris, and Jen, and to Liz Madden, Deborah Thomas, and Michelle McCay. To Sarah Arbury for helping identify the best-of, and to Molly Wyman, Jocelyn Beer, Nina Tovish, and Akela Reason for your friendship and support. I would like to thank Diane Kresh for her photographs, and Lynn Peril for her guidance as I delved into copyright research. I also appreciate the moral support and good wishes from my work buddies during this project; in particular I thank reference librarians Cassy Ammen and Jennifer Harbster for their research tips, and all the lunch partners who listened to me talk about this endlessly. I send out belly rubs to my dogs, Frieda and Felix, for keeping me sane and getting me out of the house for much-needed breaks from the computer.

The seeds of Miss Abigail were sown long ago. Thanks to my dear friend Carita Simons-Byers for letting me keep *The Art of Dating* when we parted ways that summer of 1987. Many thanks to all who have provided encouragement over the years as my alter-ego Miss Abigail was born and made a name for herself, and to the fans of MissAbigail.com, particularly those who donated books to the collection. Thanks to the thrift-list community for your friendship, humor, and endless appreciation of fun cheap stuff, and for understanding what it's like to need *just* a few more advice books.

And lastly, I am immensely grateful to all of the wonderful authors of the books in my collection. Without their work, this book would not have been possible.

Permissions

We gratefully acknowledge all those who gave permission for written and visual material to appear in this book. We made every effort to trace and contact copyright holders. If an error or omission is brought to our notice we will be pleased to remedy the situation in future editions of this book. For further information, please contact the publisher.

Excerpt from *20th-Century Teenagers*, by "A Friend of Youth." Published by the Daughters of St. Paul. Copyright 1961 by Daughters of St. Paul. Used by permission of the Daughters of St. Paul.

Allen, Betty, and Mitchell Pirie Briggs. *Mind Your Manners*. Philadelphia: J. B. Lippincott Co., 1964.

Excerpt from *The Fascinating Girl*, by Helen B. Andelin. Published by Pacific Press. Copyright 1969 and 1970 by Helen B. Andelin and Aubrey P. Andelin. Used by permission of the author.

Beery, Mary. *Manners Made Easy*. New York: McGraw-Hill Book Company, 1954.

Excerpt from *'Twixt Twelve and Twenty: Pat talks to Teenagers*, by Pat Boone. Published by Prentice-Hall, Inc. Copyright 1958 by Prentice-Hall, Inc. Used by permission of the author. Bowman, Warren D. *Home Builders of Tomorrow*. Elgin, IL: The Elgin Press, 1938.

Boykin, Eleanor. *This Way, Please: A Book of Manners*. New York: Macmillan Company, 1940.

Bruckner, P. J. *How to Give Sex Instructions*. St. Louis, MO: The Queen's Work, 1937.

Burrell, Caroline Benedict, and William Byron Forbush. *The Mother's Book*. New York: The University Society, 1919.

Crane, George W. *How to "Cash-In" on Your Worries*. Chicago: Hopkins Syndicate, 1956.

Excerpts from *Charm for Young Woman*, by Anne Culkin, Copyright 1965, Paulist Press, Inc., New York/Mahwah, N.J. Used with permission of Paulist Press.

Cummings, Edith Mae. *Pots, Pans and Millions*. Washington, D.C.: National School of Business Science for Women, 1929.

Daggett, Nancy. *Personal Beauty and Charm*. New York: The Homemaker's Encyclopedia, 1952.

Dix, Dorothy. *How to Win and Hold a Husband*. New York: Doubleday, Doran & Company, 1939.

Duvall, Evelyn Millis. *Facts of Life and Love for Teen-Agers*. New York: Association Press, 1956.

Duvall, Evelyn Millis. *The Art of Dating*. New York: Association Press, 1967.

Eaton, Crane & Pike Company. *A Desk Book on the Etiquette of Letter Writing and Social Correspondence in General*. New York: Eaton, Crane & Pike Company, 1927.

Eichler, Lillian. *Etiquette Problems in Pictures*. Oyster Bay, NY: Nelson Doubleday, 1922.

Eichler, Lillian. *Book of Etiquette*. Garden City, NY: Nelson Doubleday, 1923.

Eichler, Lillian. *Etiquette in Public, with notes on Courtship and Marriage, Book IV*. Hoboken, NJ: R. B. Davis and Company, 1924.

Elliott, Grace Loucks, and Harry Bone. *The Sex Life of Youth*. New York: Association Press, 1948. Excerpt from *Sex and the Single Man*, by Albert Ellis. Published by Lyle Stuart. Copyright 1963 by Institute for Rational Living, Inc. Used by permission of the Albert Ellis Institute.

Enright, Evelyn, and Ann Seranne. *Happy Living! A Guidebook for Brides*. Los Angeles: American Bride Publications, 1965.

Evans, C. B. S. *Man and Woman in Marriage*. Chicago: Bruce-Roberts, 1931.

Faculty of the South Philadelphia High School for Girls. *Everyday Manners for American Boys and Girls*. New York: Macmillan Company, 1923.

Farewell, Nina. *The Unfair Sex: An Exposé of the Human Male for Young Women of Most Ages*. New York: Simon and Schuster, 1953.

Fedder, Ruth. *A Girl Grows Up*. New York: McGraw-Hill Book Company, 1939.

Ford, Eileen. *Eileen Ford's A More Beautiful You in 21 Days*. New York: Simon and Schuster, 1972.

Fowler, C. H., and W. H. De Puy. *Home and Health and Home Economics*. New York: Phillips & Hunt, 1880.

Frances, Daré. *Lovely Ladies: The Art of Being a Woman*, Vol. I. Garden City, NY: Doubleday, Doran & Company, 1929.

Excerpts from *This Passion Called Love*, by Elinor Glyn. Published by The Author's Press. Copyright 1925 by The Author's Press. Used by permission of Mrs. G. Chowdharay-Best.

Excerpt from *The Philosophy of Love*, by Elinor Glyn. Published by The Author's Press. Copyright 1923 by The Author's Press. Used by permission of Mrs. G. Chowdharay-Best.

Green, W. C. *The Book of Good Manners: A Guide to Polite Usage for All Social Functions*. New York: Social Mentor Publications, 1922.

Excerpt from *Why Isn't a Nice Girl Like You Married? or, How to Get the Most out of Life While You're Single*, by Rebecca E. Greer. Published by Macmillan Company. Copyright 1969 by Rebecca Greer and the Macmillan Company. Used by permission of the author.

Griggs, Edward Howard. *Friendship, Love and Marriage*. New York: B. W. Huebsch, 1915.

Hadida, Sophie C. *Manners for Millions*. New York: Permabooks, 1950.

Hahn, Emily, and Eric Hatch. *Spousery*. New York: Franklin Watts, 1956.

Hale, Mabel. *Beautiful Girlhood*. Anderson, IN: Gospel Trumpet Co., 1922.

Haskin, Dorothy. *Just for Girls*. Grand Rapids, MI: Zondervan Publishing House, 1956.

Haupt, Enid A. *The Seventeen Book of Etiquette & Entertaining*. New York: David McKay Company, 1963.

Excerpt from *Heloise's Housekeeping Hints*, by Heloise. Published by Pocket Books. Copyright 1962 by King Features Syndicate. Used by permission of Heloise.

Hillis, Marjorie. *Live Alone and Like It: A Guide for the Extra Woman*. Indianapolis, IN: The Bobbs-Merrill Company, 1936.

Holmes, Marjorie. *I've Got to Talk to Somebody, God.* Garden City, NY: Doubleday & Co., 1969.

Hopton, Ralph Y., and Anne Balliol. *Bed Manners and Better Bed Manners.* New York: Arden Book Company, 1946.

Horton, Robert F. *On the Art of Living Together.* New York: Dodd, Mead and Company, 1896.

Hunter, Estelle B. *Personality Development: A Practical Self-Teaching Course, Unit One: Your Physical Self.* Chicago: The Better-Speech Institute of America, 1939.

Jefferis, Professor B. G. *The Household Guide, or Domestic Cyclopedia.* Atlanta, GA: J. L. Nichols & Co., 1902.

Jefferis, Professor B. G., and J. L. Nichols. *Search Lights on Health: Light on Dark Corners: A Complete Sexual Science and a Guide to Purity and Physical Manhood, Advice to Maiden, Wife and Mother, Love, Courtship and Marriage.* Naperville, IL: J. L. Nichols & Co., 1911.

Jones, Louis LeClaire. *Birthday Chats with Tomorrow's Man.* Chicago: Charles E. Tench Printing Co., 1940.

Justin, Margaret, and Lucile Rust. *Today's Home Living.* Chicago: J. B. Lippincott Company, 1947.

Kaschewski, Marjorie Roehl. *Housekeeping Made Simple.* The Homemaker's Encyclopedia, 1952.

Keller, David H. *Love, Courtship, Marriage.* New York: Roman Publishing Company, 1928.

Kellogg, J. H. *Plain Facts for Old and Young: Embracing the Natural History and Hygiene of Organic Life.* Burlington, IA: I. F. Segner, 1886.

Lane, Harriet. *The Book of Culture.* New York: Social Mentor Publications, 1922.

Lang, Barbara. *Boys and Other Beasts.* New York: Pocket Books, 1965.

Lind, G. Dallas. "An Old Practitioner." *The Mother's Guide and Daughter's Friend.* Indianapolis, IN: Normal Publishing House, 1890.

Lowry, Oscar. *A Virtuous Woman: Sex Life in Relation to the Christian Life.* Grand Rapids, MI: Zondervan Publishing House, 1938.

Excerpt from *Plain Talk! For Men Under 21!,* by Allen Ludden. Published by Dodd, Mead & Company. Copyright 1954 by Allen Ludden. Used by permission of Betty White.

Macfadden, Bernarr. *Womanhood and Marriage.* New York: Macfadden Book Company, 1923.

Magner, Rev. James A. *The Art of Happy Marriage.* Milwaukee, WI: Bruce Publishing Co., 1947.

Marbury, Elisabeth. *Manners: A Handbook of Social Customs.* Chicago: M. A. Donohue & Co., 1888.

Marshall, J. Joseph, *Living with a Husband and Liking It.* Philadelphia. Dorrance & Company, 1942.

McAndless, M. Thelma. *Manners Today.* Detroit: Briggs Publishing Company, 1943.

McDermott, Irene E., and Florence Williams Nicholas. *Living for Young Moderns.* Chicago: J. B. Lippincott Company, 1956.

Excerpt from *Your First Year of Marriage,* by Dr. Tom McGinnis. Published by Doubleday & Company. Copyright 1967 by Thomas C. McGinnis. Used by permission of Thomas C. McGinnis Jr.

Excerpt from *A Girl's Guide to Dating and Going Steady,* by Dr. Tom McGinnis. Published by Doubleday & Company. Copyright 1968 by Thomas C. McGinnis. Used by permission of Thomas C. McGinnis Jr.

Melendy, Mary Ries. *Vivilore: The Pathway to Mental and Physical Perfection.* Chicago: W. R. Vansant, 1904.

Miller, Catherine Atkinson. Eighteen: *The Art of Being a Woman.* New York: Round Table Press, 1933.

Miller, J. R. *The Wedded Life.* Philadelphia: Presbyterian Board of Publication and Sabbath School Work, 1912.

Morris, Hugh. *How to Make Love: The Secret of Wooing and Winning the One You Love,* 1936 (reprinted 1987).

Napheys, George H. *The Transmission of Life: Counsels on the Nature and Hygiene of the Masculine Function.* Philadelphia: David McKay, 1878.

Narramore, Clyde M. *Life and Love: A Christian View of Sex.* Grand Rapids, MI: Zondervan Publishing House, 1956.

New York Society of Self-Culture (eighteen authors). *Correct Social Usage.* New York: New York Society of Self-Culture, 1907.

O'Rell, Max. *Her Royal Highness Woman and His Majesty-Cupid.* New York: The Abbey Press, 1901.

Peck, Ellen. *How to Get a Teen-Age Boy and What to Do with Him When You Get Him.* New York: Bernard Geis Associates, 1969.

Pemberton, Lois. *The Stork Didn't Bring You: Sex Education for Teen-Agers.* New York: Thomas Nelson & Sons, 1965.

Pierce, Beatrice. *The Young Hostess.* New York: Farrar & Rinehart, 1938.

Pierce, V. M. *Dream Book Bridal Superstitions.* Buffalo, NY: Dr. Pierce's Invalids Hotel, ca. 1895.

Podolsky, Edward. *Sex Today in Wedded Life.* New York: Simon Publications, 1947.

Richardson, Frank Howard. *For Young Adults Only: The Doctor Discusses Your Personal Problems.* Atlanta, GA: Tupper and Love, 1961.

Rossiter, Frederick M. *The Torch of Life: A Key to Sex Harmony.* New York: Eugenics Publishing Co., 1932.

Ruth, John A. *Decorum: A Practical Treatise on Etiquette and Dress of the Best American Society.* New York: Union Publishing House, 1880.

Sanger, Margaret. *Happiness in Marriage.* Garden City, NY: Blue Ribbon Books, 1940.

Sangster, Margaret E. *The Art of Home Making.* New York: Christian Herald Bible House, 1898.

Scanzoni, Letha. *Youth Looks at Love.* Westwood, NJ: Fleming H. Revell Company, 1965.

Excerpts from *The Art of Making a Perfect Husband,* by "A Husband" [Cyril Scott]. Published by Harper & Brothers Publishers. Copyright 1929 by Harper & Brothers Publishers. Used by permission of Desmond Scott.

Scott, James Foster. *The Sexual Instinct: Its Use and Dangers as Affecting Heredity and Morals.* New York: E. B. Treat & Company, 1899.

Shannon, Professor T. W. *Nature's Secrets Revealed: Scientific Knowledge of the Laws of Sex Life and Heredity, or Eugenics.* Marietta, OH: The S. A. Mullikin Company, 1916.

Sproat, Nancy. *The School of Good Manners.* New York: Samuel Wood & Sons, 1822. (Reprint: David Marshall, Carthage, Indiana, 1888.)

Strain, Frances Bruce. *Teen Days: A Book for Boys and Girls*. New York: D. Appleton-Century Company, 1946.

Thomas, Kay. *Secrets of Loveliness*. New York: Scholastic Book Services, 1969.

Tolman, Ruth. *Charm and Poise for Getting Ahead*. New York: Milady Publishing Co., 1967.

Excerpts from *The Cool Book: A Teen-Ager's Guide to Survival in a Square Society*, by Art Unger. Published by Monarch Books. Copyright 1961 by Arthur Unger. Used by permission of Victoria Irwin.

Van Duzer, Adelaide Laura, Edna M. Andrix, Ethelwyn L. Bobenmyer & others. Edited by Benjamin R. Andrews. *Everyday Living for Girls*. Chicago: J. B. Lippincott Company, 1936.

Van Evera, Jean. *How to Be Happy While Single*. Philadelphia: J. B. Lippincott Co., 1949.

Walker, Mrs. A. *Female Beauty, as Preserved and Improved by Regimen, Cleanliness and Dress*. New York: Scofield and Voorhies, 1840.

Excerpt from *How to Pick Up Girls!*, by Eric Weber. Published by Symphony Press. Copyright 1970 by Eric Weber. Used by permission of the author.

Whitman, Jason. *The Young Lady's Aid, to Usefulness and Happiness*. Portland, ME: S. H. Colesworthy, 1838.

Wilcox, Ella Wheeler. *Men, Women and Emotions*. Chicago: W. B. Conkey Company, 1897.

Wilson, Margery. *Pocket Book of Etiquette*. New York: Pocket Books, 1940.

Wilson, Margery. *The Woman You Want to Be*. Philadelphia: J. B. Lippincott Co., 1942.

Wolfe, W. Béran. *A Woman's Best Years: The Art of Staying Young*. Garden City, NY: Garden City Publishing Co., 1946.

Zenner, Philip. *Education in Sexual Physiology and Hygiene: A Physician's Message*. Cincinnati, OH: Robert Clarke Company, 1910.

Illustrations

Pg. 4. Photograph of young couple (ca. 1960) courtesy of Linda Salisbury.

Pg. 7. Illustration of "Chas. E. Blaney's Big Extravaganza: A Boy Wanted," from Theatrical

Poster Collection, Library of Congress, Prints and Photographs Division, Call Number POS - TH - 1898 .B69.

Pg. 12. Illustration (front cover) of *Growing Up*, 2nd ed., by Roy O. Billett and J. Wendell Yeo. Published by D. C. Heath and Company, 1958.

Pg. 16. Illustration of woman in bra from *Secrets of Love and Marriage*, by James Parker Hendry and E. Podolsky, ed. Published by Herald Publishing Company, 1939.

Pg. 19. Illustration (front cover) of *How to Give Sex Instructions*, by P. J. Bruckner, S. J. Published by The Queen's Work, 1937.

Pg. 25. Illustration of "Am I Ready for School Today?," from the Cleanliness Institute. Published by the Cleanliness Institute, New York, undated.

Pg. 27. Photograph of group of young people in pyramid pile (ca. 1930s) courtesy of Linda Salisbury.

Pg. 34. Illustration of the wallflower at a party, from *Etiquette Problems in Pictures*, by Lillian Eichler. Published by Nelson Doubleday, Inc., 1922.

Pg. 37. Illustration of "A Bashful Beau," from *Nature's Secrets Revealed: Scientific Knowledge of the Laws of Sex Life and Heredity, or Eugenics*, by Professor T. W. Shannon. Published by The S. A. Mullikin Company, 1916.

Pg. 44. Illustration (front cover) of *How to Pick Up Girls!*, by Eric Weber. Published by Symphony Press. Copyright 1970 by Eric Weber. Used by permission of the author.

Pg. 47. Photograph of "He Loves Me, He Loves Me Not," by E. W. Kelley. Copyright 1906. From Library of Congress, Prints and Photographs Division, LC-USZ62-64041.

Pg. 55. Photograph of "When Love Is Young," by E. W. Kelley. Copyright 1906. From Library of Congress, Prints & Photographs Division, LC-USZ62-64049.

Pg. 60. Illustration of "The Rustic Coquette," from *Vivilore: The Pathway to Mental and Physical Perfection*, by Dr. Mary Ries Melendy. Published by W. R. Vansant, 1904.

Pg. 63. Photograph of "Making a Favorable Impression," by Melander & Bro. Copyright 1880. From Library of Congress, Prints & Photographs Division, LC-USZ62-56658.

Pg. 71. Photograph of girl brushing her teeth, from *Growing Up*, 2nd ed., by Roy O. Billett and J. Wendell Yeo. Published by D. C. Heath and Company, 1958.

Pg. 74. Illustration of "Marie," from *Vivilore: The Pathway to Mental and Physical Perfection*, by Dr. Mary Ries Melendy. Published by W. R. Vansant, 1904.

Pg. 75. Photograph of group of women looking at magazine courtesy of Linda Salisbury.

Pg. 85. Illustration (front cover) of *Plain Talk! For Men Under 21!*, by Allen Ludden. Published by Dodd, Mead & Company. Copyright 1954 by Allen Ludden. Used by permission of Betty White.

Pg. 94. Photograph of kids at a dance, from *Growing Up*, 2nd ed., by Roy O. Billett and J. Wendell Yeo. Published by D. C. Heath and Company, 1958.

Pg. 98. Illustration (front cover) of *A Virtuous Woman: Sex Life in Relation to the Christian Life*, by Oscar Lowry. Published by Zondervan Publishing House, 1938.

Pg. 98. Illustration (front cover) of *The Way of a Man with a Maid*, by Oscar Lowry. Published by Zondervan Publishing House, 1940.

Pg. 102. Illustration of woman eating corn and demonstrating good table manners, from *The Book of Good Manners: A Guide to Polite Usage for All Social Functions*, by W. C. Green. Published by Social Mentor Publications, 1922.

Pg. 105. Illustration of "Talking Before Marriage," from *Search Lights on Health: Light on Dark Corners: A Complete Sexual Science and a Guide to Purity and Physical Manhood, Advice to Maiden, Wife and Mother, Love, Courtship and Marriage*, by B. G. Jefferis and J. L. Nichols. Published by J. L. Nichols & Co. Copyright 1911.

Pg. 107. Illustration of "Hasty Familiarity is Fraught with Many Dangers," from *Search Lights on Health: Light on Dark Corners: A Complete Sexual Science and a Guide to Purity and Physical Manhood, Advice to Maiden, Wife and Mother, Love, Courtship and Marriage*, by B. G. Jefferis and J. L. Nichols. Published by J. L. Nichols & Co. Copyright 1911.

Pg. 107. Illustration (front cover) of *'Twixt Twelve and Twenty: Pat talks to Teenagers*, by Pat Boone. Published by Prentice-Hall, Inc. Copyright 1958 by Prentice-Hall, Inc. Used by permission of the author.

Pg. 110. Photograph of "Blissful Moments," by R. Y. Young, American Stereoscopic Co., Copyright 1896. Library of Congress, Prints & Photographs Division, LC-USZ62-75652.

Pg. 121. Photograph of "Woman Between Two Admirers," by Fritz W. Guerin. No date. Library of Congress, Prints & Photographs Division, LC-USZ62-74324.

Pg. 128. Illustration (front cover) of *The Art of Dating*, by Evelyn Millis Duvall. Published by Association Press. Copyright 1967.

Pg. 134. Photograph of "A Maiden's Dream—How Sweet is That?" by E. W. Kelley. Copyright 1906. Library of Congress, Prints & Photographs Division, LC-USZ62-64046.

Pg. 140. Photograph of "On Vengeance Bent, the Wrathful Lover Started, While Fannie Hid Her Face Quite Broken-Hearted," by Keystone View Company. Copyright 1906. Library of Congress, Prints & Photographs Division, LC-USZ62-100436.

Pg. 142. Illustration of "A Rejected Lover," from *Search Lights on Health: Light on Dark Corners: A Complete Sexual Science and a Guide to Purity and Physical Manhood, Advice to Maiden, Wife and Mother, Love, Courtship and Marriage*, by B. G. Jefferis and J. L. Nichols. Published by J. L. Nichols & Co. Copyright 1911.

Pg. 148. Illustration of "Busy and Happy," from *Vivilore: The Pathway to Mental and Physical Perfection*, by Dr. Mary Ries Melendy. Published by W. R. Vansant, 1904.

Pg. 150. Illustration of "Dreaming of the Future," from *Nature's Secrets Revealed: Scientific Knowledge of the Laws of Sex Life and Heredity, or Eugenics*, by Professor T. W. Shannon. Published by the S. A. Mullikin Company. Copyright 1916.

Pg. 156. Illustration (front cover) of *Live Alone and Like It: A Guide for the Extra Woman*, by Marjorie Hillis. Published by The Bobbs-Merrill Company. Copyright 1936.

Pg. 162. Photograph of "A Whole day's Catch—'We didn't fish quite all the time,'" by E. W. Kelley. Copyright 1906. Library of Congress, Prints & Photographs Division, LC-USZ62-64048.

Pg. 170. Illustration (front cover) of *How to Win and Hold a Husband*, by Dorothy Dix. Published by Doubleday, Doran & Company. Copyright 1939.

Pg. 175. Photograph of "A Soul Kiss," no identified photographer or publisher. Copyright 1909. Library of Congress, Prints & Photographs Division, LC-USZ62-65700.

Pg. 177. Illustration of "Love's Missive," from *Nature's Secrets Revealed: Scientific Knowledge of the Laws of Sex Life and Heredity, or Eugenics*, by Professor T. W. Shannon. Published by the S. A. Mullikin Company. Copyright 1916.

Pg. 184. Illustration of "The Pledge of Love and Honor," from *Vivilore: The Pathway to Mental and Physical Perfection*, by Dr. Mary Ries Melendy. Published by W. R. Vansant, 1904.

Pg. 188. Photograph of "Sovereigns of Love's Domain," by E. W. Kelley. Copyright 1906. Library of Congress, Prints & Photographs Division, LC-USZ62-64055.

Pg. 196. Photograph of "The Toast to the Bride," by C. L. Wasson, International View Co. Copyright 1905. Library of Congress, Prints & Photographs Division, LC-USZ62-67615.

Pg. 199. Illustration (front cover) of *Dream Book Bridal Superstitions*, by V. M. Pierce. Published by Dr. Pierce's Invalids Hotel, ca. 1895.

Pg. 201. Photograph of gift card "A gift for your wedding" (ca. 1930s) courtesy of Linda Salisbury.

Pg. 206. Photograph of "Alone, at Last Alone," by C. L. Wasson, International View Co. Copyright 1905. Library of Congress, Prints & Photographs Division, LC-USZ62-63301.

Pg. 209. Illustration (front cover) of *Bed Manners and Better Bed Manners*, by Ralph Y. Hopton and Anne Balliol. Published by Arden Book Company. Copyright 1946.

Pg. 212. Photograph of "Slow! Well I'll Beat You Yet," by E. W. Kelley. Copyright 1906. Library of Congress, Prints & Photographs Division, LC-USZ62-64061.

Pg. 216. Sealy Advertisement "Advice to Single Girls on Furnishing a double bedroom," appearing in *Happy Living! A Guidebook for Brides*, by Evelyn Enright and Ann Seranne. Published by American Bride Publications. Copyright 1965 by American Bride Publications. Used by permission of Sealy Company.

Pg. 223. Illustration of woman ironing from *Housekeeping Made Simple*, by Marjorie Roehl Kaschewski. Published by The Homemaker's Encyclopedia. Copyright 1952.

Pg. 226. Photograph of "Take your time Mr. Peck—Haste Makes Waste," by E. W. Kelley. Copyright 1906. Library of Congress, Prints & Photographs Division, LC-USZ62-64063.

Pg. 232. Illustration (front and back cover) of *Spousery*, by Emily Hahn and Eric Hatch. Published by Franklin Watts. Copyright 1956.

Pg. 235. Illustration (front cover) of *Living with a Husband and Liking It*, by J. Joseph Marshall. Published by Dorrance & Company. Copyright 1942.

Pg. 244. Illustration (front cover) of *Happiness for Husbands and Wives*, by Harold Shryock. Published by Review and Herald. Copyright 1949.

Pg. 245. Photograph of happy couple courtesy of Linda Salisbury.

About the Author

H aunted by a charm-school class in junior high school and the inability to do her own hair or apply makeup, Miss Abigail (also known as Abigail Grotke) has been collecting classic advice books for over twenty years. She has an extensive background in print and digital publications and a keen interest in historical materials and pop culture, not to mention a love of crawling around dirty used bookstores to find the perfect book to add to her collection. She has combined selections of advice from her books with witty commentary to create her award-winning Web site, Miss Abigail's Time Warp Advice, and a high-profile weekly column for the *London Times Magazine* from September 2001 through February 2003. During the day, she is a digital projects coordinator at the Library of Congress, and has previously worked in the publications office of the Smithsonian American Art Museum. In 2004 she was named one of *Library Journal*'s "Movers and Shakers," an annual feature which sets out to identify "emerging leaders in the Library world." She lives in an old house in Takoma Park, Maryland, with her terrier mutts, Frieda and Felix, and her amazing collection of ice crushers.